In or Out: Does It Matter?
An Evidence-Based Analysis of the
Euro's Trade Effects

Centre for Economic Policy Research (CEPR)

Centre for Economic Policy Research
90-98 Goswell Road
London EC1V 7RR
UK

Tel: +44 (0)20 7878 2900
Fax: +44 (0)20 7878 2999
Email: cepr@cepr.org
Website: www.cepr.org

British Library Cataloguing in Publication Data
A catalogue record for this book is available from the British Library

ISBN: 1 898128 91 X

In or Out: Does It Matter?
An Evidence-Based Analysis of the Euro's Trade Effects

Richard Baldwin, Graduate Institute of International Studies, Geneva and CEPR

This report has been financed by the Economic and Social Research Council (ESRC) through the EvidenceNetwork project. The views expressed do not represent those of the ESRC, CEPR or any of the other funding organisations mentioned but of the author alone.

Centre for Economic Policy Research (CEPR)

About the Author

Richard Baldwin has been Professor of International Economics at the Graduate Institute of International Studies since 1991, Policy Director of CEPR since 2006 and Chairman of the Foundation Board of the World Trade Institute in Bern since 2004. He was a Managing Editor of the journal Economic Policy from 2000 to 2005 and Programme Director of CEPR's International Trade programme from 1991 to 2001. Before coming to Geneva, he was Senior Staff Economist for the President's Council of Economic Advisors in the Bush Administration (1990-91) and Associate Professor at Columbia University Business School, having done his PhD in economics at MIT with Paul Krugman (1986), his Masters with Alasdair Smith at LSE (1981) and first degree with Andre Sapir (1980). He taught the PhD trade course at MIT in 2002-03 and has been a visiting professor at universities in Italy, Sweden, Germany and Norway. He has also worked as a consultant for the ECB, European Commission, OECD, the World Bank, EFTA, USAID and UNCTAD. He is the author of numerous books and articles, including the CEPR book Towards an Integrated Europe, published in 1994. His research interests include international trade, regionalism (most recently East Asian regionalism) and European integration.

Dedication: To my father, Robert Edward Baldwin, who taught me how to think like an economist.

Acknowledgements

I would like to thank Nadia Rocha and Virginia Di Nino for assistance with data-wrestling, theory-checking and proofreading. Virginia has downloaded literally tens of millions of data points for this book and our joint work. Nadia helped me with the review of the Rose effect literature and the trade pricing literature; she also worked out the impact of lower market-entry costs in a three-country setting (as part of her thesis). I thank Andy Rose, Volker Nitsch, Howard Wall, Alejandro Micco, and Hakan Nordström for providing excellent comments and answering many questions about their data and regressions. They saw early drafts of Chapters 2 and 3 and eliminated several mistakes. Many researchers sent me data that I have used in the figure, tables or regressions. The list includes Stefano Tarantola, Andy Rose, Volker Nitsch, Howard Wall, Alejandro Micco, Hakan Nordström, Jan Fidrmuc, and Francesco Mongelli. Daria Taglioni has helped me enormously with checking the gravity model econometrics. Some of the book's elements build on my earlier articles and I would like to thank my co-authors (in various combinations) of those articles: Bob Anderton, Frauke Skuderlny and Daria Taglioni.

Charles Wyploz, Andre Sapir and Thierry Mayer read an early complete draft of the book and provided extremely helpful comments and critiques. I am especially indebted to Charles for some late night editing/advice on the final chapter on policy implications.

An early draft of Chapter 2 and some of Chapter 3 was presented at the ECB in June 2005. Jeffery Frankel and Jacques Melitz were my discussants. Their insightful comments produced many improvements that have been included in this book. I would like to thank the ECB, especially Otto Issing and Francesco Mongelli for getting me to write that paper. The paper for the ECB conference and the Frankel and Melitz comments were published, after a long delay, as Baldwin (2006). Special thanks are extended to Francesco Mongelli who carefully read the first complete draft of my ECB paper and caught many typos, thinkos and omissions. Philip Lane provided many useful pointers for my ECB paper, especially on the endogeneity of currency unions.

Contents

List of Figures

List of Tables

Foreword

CEPR hosts a node in the Economic and Social Research Council's EvidenceNetwork initiative, which aims to advance the methodology of evidence-based policy (EBP) assessment and to apply it to a wide range of policy issues. The CEPR node is called the Centre for Comparative European Policy Evaluation, and its aim is to consider cross-country evidence as the basis for assessing the impact of, and opportunities for economic policy. The Centre addresses policy issues that involve decision-making at the EU level as well as UK policy issues for which the experiences of other European countries are relevant and where comparative work across countries is likely to prove illuminating. This fourth report from the Centre, written by Professor Richard Baldwin, aims to establish a consensus estimate of the euro's impact on trade flows.

The opinions expressed herein are those of the author alone, and do not reflect the views of the institution to which he is affiliated, the Economic and Social Research Council,or of CEPR, which takes no institutional policy positions. The Centre is, however, delighted to provide the author this forum for presentation of a subject that has important implications for both members and non-members of the euro area.

Stephen Yeo
Chief Executive Officer, CEPR

March 2006

Executive Summary

Economics played little role in the decision to create the euro – politics was king. Going forward, however, economics moves to centre stage. Should the euro area worry about admitting new members who are very economically different from incumbents? What are the costs and benefits of euro adoption for potential joiners? Are the famous Maastricht Criteria the right economic tests for potential members? How worried should the European Central Bank be about unsynchronised booms and busts in the euro area?

The microeconomic effects of the euro are at the heart of these questions since they determine the extent to which euro usage will foster economic integration among incumbents and joiners. Two microeconomic effects are critical – the impact on international capital flows, and the impact on international goods flows, i.e. trade. The focus here is on the trade flows.

This report marshals the best available empirical evidence on the size and nature of the euro's pro-trade effect. Six main findings are extracted from the empirical research:

1) The pro-trade effect of the euro is modest – somewhere between 5% and 15%, with 9% being the best estimate.

2) It happened very quickly, appearing in 1999.

3) It was not exclusive; euro-usage boosted imports from non-euro area nations almost as much as it boosted imports from euro area partners, i.e. there was no trade diversion but rather external trade creation in addition to the internal trade creation. The best estimate of the external trade creation is 7%. The best empirical evidence suggests that this applies only the euro area imports, but some evidence suggests that it applies to euro area exports as well.

4) It involved little or no convergence in euro area prices despite the jump in trade flows.

5) New research in this report suggests that reduced transaction costs were not primarily responsible for the pro-trade effects, arguing instead that it was caused by the export of new goods to euro area economies. The mechanism driving this may have been a reduction in the fixed cost of introducing new goods into euro area markets. This mechanism, which is tantamount to a unilateral product-market liberalisation, would account for the lack of trade diversion (it would stimulate the introduction of new goods from euro area-based and non-euro area-based exporters alike) and it would account for the jump up in trade without price convergence (total volumes can rise at constant prices).

6) The pro-trade effect varies a great deal across nations; Spain seems to have been the biggest gainer while Greece's gain is estimated to be nil or even negative.

7) The pro-trade effect varies greatly across sectors, with the gains concentrated in increasing-returns-to-scale sectors such as machinery & transport equipment, and chemicals. Beverages & tobacco was the biggest gainer, but this may be due to spurious factors (VAT fraud).

The policy implications of these findings are grouped into two broad categories – lessons for potential joiners and lessons for the euro area's 12 members and its economic management.

Why trade effects matter for potential joiners

The costs and benefits of joining the euro area are easy, according to traditional thinking (i.e. 'optimal currency area' reasoning). The costs are on the macroeconomic side. By embracing the ECB's one-size-fits-all policy, the joiner foregoes a monetary policy tailored to its national stabilisation needs. The benefits are on the microeconomic side. Adopting the euro area's currency means tighter economic integration with a bloc that constitutes one-sixth of world output and 30% of world trade. But how much will the common currency boost trade if you do join? How much 'trade diversion' will you suffer if you don't join?

The potential joiners fall into two groups – the medium to small sized economies (Britain, Sweden, Poland, Denmark, Czech Republic and Hungary), and the minuscule economies (Slovenia, Slovakia, Estonia, Latvia, Lithuania, Cyprus and Malta).

A weaker economic case for joining the euro: Britain, Sweden and Denmark

The small overall size of the pro-trade effect and the lack of trade diversion weaken both the economic case and the political economy case for British, Swedish and Danish membership in the euro area. Here is the argument.

The traditional 'optimal currency area' framework is relevant for medium and small economies, especially Britain, Sweden and Denmark. Their economic-management institutions can run effective monetary policies and their economies are large enough to warrant nationally-tailored monetary policies, at least on occasion, so joining entails a macroeconomic cost. This should be balanced by a microeconomic gain. The UK Treasury's 2003 study on Britain's readiness to join, for example, suggests that the microeconomic gains from using the euro may be large due mainly to a large pro-trade effect (assumed to be over 40%). This large number was based on empirical research that has subsequently been discredited, as this report argues at length (Chapter 2). If the real pro-trade effect is just 9% the microeconomic gains will be modest. Moreover, since the euro has produced 'external trade creation' much of the trade gain – the extra exports to euro area nations – has already occurred and the gain to Britain, Sweden and Denmark from adopting the euro are correspondingly reduced (on exports, joiners only get the difference between the internal and external trade creation effects, not the full 9%). In short, the lack of trade diversion means that the economic case for forming the euro area in the first place is quite different from the case for joining it now.

Politics versus economics

This report's findings also suggest a sharp division between the political-economy gains and the economic gains. Greater exports are a political-economy 'prize' that should ease the political 'sacrifice' on the stabilisation side. But the modest size of the pro-trade effect means this prize will be small. The lack of trade diversion means that export losses from staying out will be nil. In other words, staying outside the euro area is not like staying out of a preferential trade area. Continuing with the political-economy mercantilist thinking, the big export winners from UK, Swedish and Danish membership would be exporters in the euro area nations who would see their exports to newcomers rise by 9%.

The case for joining the miniscule economies: Estonia, Latvia, Lithuania, Slovenia, Cyprus and Malta

Traditional costs-benefit analysis does not apply to many of the new members of the EU. These nations are so small that the macroeconomic cost of embracing the euro is not a cost at all. As Andres Sutt, deputy governor of the Bank of Estonia, phrased the point: '... you can't cook a different soup in one corner of the pot.' The GDPs of the six nations most eager to join are smaller than Luxembourg's – indeed, their economies are smaller than that of a good-sized French city. Just as issuing extra currency in Dijon would do little to stimulate the local economy, pursuing an independent monetary policy in Estonia would do little good. And it could do a lot of harm by opening the door to foreign exchange crises.

For these nations, the modest size of the euro's pro-trade effect is basically irrelevant. The finding of external trade creation, however, implies that the costs of waiting are not as high as they would be if staying out entailed trade diversion. For the euro area incumbents, however, the modest trade effects means that one cannot rely on massive increases in trade to bring these nations' economies into synch with the euro area average. This brings us to the policy implications for the euro area's political and economic managers.

Implications for the ECB and euro area members: not a silver bullet

Although monetary union was about politics, not economics, one recent line of thinking has cast economics in the role of facilitator. This thinking – the so-called 'endogenous optimal currency area' reasoning – argues that monetary union produces tighter economic integration within the bloc and this makes the ECB's one-size-fits-all monetary policy more appropriate for each of the euro area economies. The pro-trade effect of the euro was one of the key mechanisms suggested. It argues that the pro-trade effects helps harmonise national business cycles via, for example, 'demand spillovers' (booming demand in one nation would result in a rapid rise in imports which would in turn stimulate output in other euro area nations).

Plainly this thinking – if it were true – would be very attractive to policy makers in the euro area, the ECB and those Member States who want to join fast. To reform-weary national policy makers in the euro area, this analysis would imply that trade creation is an easy way to harmonise the euro area economically (structural and labour market reforms being the hard way). To potential euro-adopters, it would imply that they need not adjust before joining since trade creation will do the job after joining. To ECB monetary policy deciders, it would hold out the hope that their jobs will get easier.

Alas, the premise is false – at least as far as the trade channel is concerned. This thinking might have been important if the pro-trade effects were as large as the early literature suggested, e.g. Rose (2000a). Chapter 2 argues that these large effects were the product of mistaken statistical analysis and that they should be ignored for policy making purposes. The best-estimate of the pro-trade effect is quite modest, so the endogenous-OCA arguments based on trade creation are of second-order importance. Of course, other channels such as financial market integration and changes in wage formation processes may still be important empirically.

Implications for prospective monetary unions in the rest of the world

The European Union is held up as an ideal of how tight economic integration promotes the welfare of citizens and brings peace among former enemies. To the extent that the logic of 'one market, one money' holds true, the path to tighter economic integration leads inevitably to the question of a common currency. Indeed, just as the calls for a monetary union in Europe were strengthened by the currency turbulence in Europe in the 1990s, the 1997 Asian Crisis and various Latin American currency crises have lead to a keen interest of the economics of common currencies. The lessons of this report for other regions of the world are that a common currency provides a modest boost to trade integration, but at least for Europe, it has not been a 'silver bullet.'

Caveat Emptor

With just six years of post-euro data, it is impossible to think that the empirical work reviewed and presented in this book will be the last word on the subject. Future experience may revise the findings, and will certainly provide a better understanding of the economic mechanism through which the euro has affected trade. But one must stop somewhere. After all, books are never done, they're just due. Given the impending enlargements of the euro area, this seemed a good time for stocktaking.

1 Introduction

Just at the end of the twentieth century – a century that witnessed Europeans killing Europeans on an industrial scale – something strange happened. Three hundred million Europeans abandoned their familiar francs, marks, guilders and shillings and adopted a made-up currency. They then turned over macroeconomic stabilization for a sixth of the world's economy to a made-up central bank. This was a brave step. Things turned out well economically and politically but this was not obvious beforehand. Truth be told, economists could only guess at what the economic impact would be. Even now we are still working out what happened. This report's aim is to contribute to this ongoing 'what happened' effort.

The report focuses on the trade effects of the euro.

This may seem a narrow topic – most books on the euro touch on everything from inflation psychology and supermarket pricing schemes to corporate debt markets and central bank governance. While narrow, the euro's trade effect is a topic that is both critical to policy choices and amenable to evidence-based research.

Critical to policy choices

The euro was created for political reasons. Economics – especially the trade effects – was a minor issue in the minds of the men and women who launched Europe's monetary union. Going forward, however, economic issues play a much more central role. What are the costs and benefits of euro-adoption for potential joiners? Should the euro area worry about letting in new members who are very economically different to incumbents? Are the famous Maastricht Criteria, which were used in setting up the euro area the right tests for potential members? How worried should the European Central Bank be about unsynchronized booms and busts in the euro area?

At the heart of all these questions lie the microeconomic effects of the euro, especially the extent to which the euro fosters economic integration among its members. Two effects are critical – the impact of the euro on international flows of capital and capital markets, and the impact of the euro on international flows of goods and goods markets, i.e. trade. This book focuses on the latter.

Amenable to evidence-based research

Five years ago, empirical research on the trade effects of currency arrangements was catapulted from one of the deepest cellars of academic obscurity to one of the most active issues in empirical international economics. The underlying cause was the emergence of vast international datasets and the empirical tools to use them, but the proximate cause was a celebrated paper by Berkeley economist Andrew Rose which claimed that a common currency boosted bilateral trade by 200%. Since then a broad range of economists have marshalled a broad range of techniques and datasets to investigate the 'Rose effect' more thoroughly. Very recently, empirical researchers have begun to ask more pointed questions focused on the nature of the pro-trade effects rather than simply estimating its overall magnitude. Which sectors and which countries are most affected? By which economic mechanisms does a common currency affect trade flows and trade pricing? This recent and rapid emergence of empirical work suggests that the time is ripe for a critical review and synthesis of the evidence-based research.

The report's organization

The first two-fifths of the report systematically sort through the existing empirical literature – a task that is necessary since existing estimates of a currency union's impact on trade are all over the place. Some authors claim that currency unions boost trade by more 1000%; others find no effect or even a negative effect. To provide a structure for evaluating the broad range of estimates, Chapter 2 also presents a theory-based analysis of the econometrics of the gravity model (the backbone of the empirical literature) and uses this to point out many systematic errors in the literature on European and non-European currency unions.

Chapter 3 considers a number of detailed data problems that may imply that the Rose effect is a statistical illusion. There is no way to be absolutely sure how important these data problems are, but it is important to highlight the data limitations.

The next task is the report's heart, so to speak. Chapter 4 extracts the stylized empirical facts from the existing literature, being careful to discard results from the many studies that are vitiated by serious econometric errors. It then goes on to do a bit of Sherlock Holmes-ing. It considers a number of possible explanations and finds that many of them are at odds with some or all of the stylized facts. The one possibility that seems consistent with all the facts is the 'new goods hypothesis', the notion that the euro boosted the range of products that were exported to euro area nations by both euro area and non-euro area nations. The economics of this sort of effect can be tricky. Indeed, until the so-called 'new new' trade theory got started with Melitz (2003), trade economists did not have the tools to analyze carefully the logic of such effects.

Chapter 5 presents some *de novo* empirical evidence that supports the new goods hypothesis. Chapter 6 sums up the report's findings and discusses the policy implications.

2   Literature Review

This chapter provides a critical and synthetic review of the empirical literature on the pro-trade effects of adopting a common currency. The first section considers the pre-euro literature. The second section considers empirical studies that focus on the euro. We start, however, by putting the literature into a historical context. On the currency-trade link issue economists were right, then they were wrong, and now they are right again.

A puzzling non-result

For more than a hundred years, received wisdom held that stable international exchange rates were essential to international trade. This belief was based largely on the correlation between favourable trade performance and adherence to the gold standard. As the leading gold-standard scholar Michael Bordo puts it: 'The period from 1880 to 1914 is known as the classical gold standard. During that time the majority of countries adhered (in varying degrees) to gold. It was also a period of unprecedented economic growth with relatively free trade in goods, labour, and capital.'[1]

This received wisdom, however, was most definitely not an 'evidence-based' policy analysis. From the time computers became widely available to economists in the 1970s right up to the year 2000, economists failed to find a robust, evidence-based link between exchange rate volatility and trade.

This was not for want of trying.

The IMF was set up in the 1940s to help fix exchange rates worldwide. When its raison d'être – the Bretton Woods fixed exchange rate system – collapsed in the early 1970s, IMF economists set about 'proving' that exchange rate volatility would harm world trade. Despite a massive effort, no clear-cut evidence could be found linking volatility and trade flows (IMF, 1984). Some authors found the link to be negative, others positive, but most found no statistically significant link at all. When I reviewed the literature in 1990 for a background study that I wrote for the European Commission's report *One Market, One Money*, active research on the topic was dead in the water.[2] The state of the art was summarized in the title of the 1991 paper by Lorenzo Bini Smaghi, 'Exchange Rate Variability and International Trade: Why is it so Difficult to Find any Empirical Relationship?'[3]

Even with radically more sophisticated empirical techniques and an extra decade worth of data, economists in the mid-1990s could find no link. For example, a famous 1993 paper by Jeffery Frankel and Shang-Jin Wei asserted, '...if real exchange rate volatility in Europe were to double, the volume of intra-regional trade might fall by an estimated 0.7%'.

This three-decade old failure to find empirical support for the received wisdom led to a sort of 'cognitive dissonance' in the profession. It is summed up in the first sentence of an article Shang-Jin Wei published in late 1999:

A puzzle in empirical international finance is the difficulty in identifying a large and negative effect of exchange rate volatility on trade. This has led to a bifurcation of reactions. On the one hand, policy circles choose to ignore this literature, and continue to believe that exchange rate volatility has a large and negative effect on goods trade. For example, government officials in Europe explicitly and repeatedly cite this effect as a primary justification for the European Monetary System and the drive for a single currency in Europe. On the other hand, clever economists start to think of clever explanations for why the effect should be small on a conceptual level.

All this was to change the year after Wei's article appeared.

2.1   The Rose vine: review of the pre-euro literature

Andy Rose of the University of California-Berkeley opened a new chapter in international economics with an *Economic Policy* article published in 2000. Rose (2000a) asked a simple question and got a simple answer:

> What is the effect of a common currency on international trade? Answer: Large.

In fact Rose (2000a) asserted that a currency union would increase trade 200% and this was on top of the large and negative impact he found for exchange rate volatility.

Given the 25 years of futile searching described above, it is easy to understand why Rose's paper was nothing short of a revolution. Much of the response has been critical, with authors trying to reduce the size of the impact. This section reviews the evidence on the trade effects of currency unions – what I'll call the Rose effect for brevity's sake – on the pre-euro data. The next section reviews the evidence on the trade effects of the euro itself.

As an aside, I want to thank Andy for introducing a tradition of jocular writing into this literature. The final version that Andy turned in to Charles Wyplosz (the Managing Editor of *Economic Policy* who did the final editing; David Begg handled the manuscript in its early stages) was chock-a-block full of exuberant English. Charles tempered some of the most avant-garde constructions, but the published version of Rose (2000a) is still a lot of fun to read. Volker Nitsch seconded this with his papers entitled: 'Honey I Shrunk the Currency Union Effect' and 'Have a Break'; I shall struggle to uphold the tradition in reviewing the literature.

Scientific rectitude

Andy Rose is also responsible for another remarkable feature of this literature – transparency and scientific rectitude. All of Rose's datasets and regressions are posted on his website. This has permitted scholars from around the world to check his data and results, tinker with specifications and challenge his findings. Subsequent contributors to this literature have generally followed this stellar example.

Organization of the pre-euro literature review

This section provides a 'guided tour' of the origins, core methodologies and principal findings of the empirical literature on pre-euro Rose effects. It is arranged in approximate chronological order. An early version of this chapter was presented at a June 2005 conference at the ECB; Jeffery Frankel and Jacques Melitz were my discussants and I thank them for the valuable comments and critiques.[4]

2.1.1 Roots: the world through Rose coloured glasses

Rose (2000)a started the debate with his finding that countries in a currency union traded three times more with each other than one would expect. He arrived at that astonishing result using a gravity-equation approach on data for bilateral trade among 186 nations.[5] His cross-section regression was:

$$\ln(RV_{od}) = a_0 + \beta_1\ln(RY_oRY_d) + \beta_2\ln(\text{Distance}_{od}) + \beta_3(CU_{od}) + \text{controls}$$

where RV is the real value of bilateral trade, the RYs are real GDPs of the origin nation (*o* is a mnemonic for origin) and destination nation (*d* is a mnemonic for origin), and CU is a dummy that switches on when nations *o* and *d* share a common currency. In his favourite regression, $\beta_3 = 1.21$ which implies trade between common-currency pairs was $e^{1.21} = 3.35$ times larger than the baseline model would suggest. That means sharing a common currency boosts trade by 235%.

The size of this common-currency effect was far too large to be believed and the profession's assault on this claim began even before he presented it at the October 1999 Economic Policy Panel that was hosted by the Bank of Finland. There were three main themes in these critiques:

- Omitted variables (omitting variables that are pro-trade and correlated with the CU dummy biases the estimate upwards).

- Reverse causality (large bilateral trade flows cause a common currency rather than vice versa).

- Model mis-specification.

Figure 2.1 Hub and spoke common currency arrangements

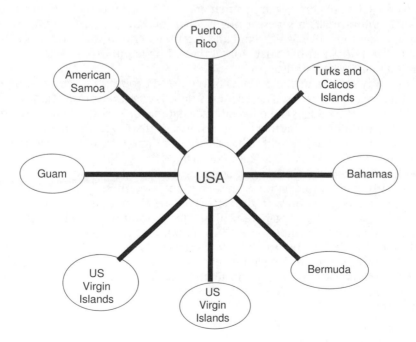

Most critiques turned on the fact that most of the common currency pairs involved nations that were very small and very poor. A highly readable early presentation of such critiques can be found in Nitsch (2002).

In his revisions, Rose produced a battery of robustness checks that he claimed had repulsed each of these critiques, leaving his central result essentially unaltered. As the Editors' Introduction to the issue in which Rose (2000a) appears says: 'The Panel admired the paper and the author's thoroughness but retained an uneasy feeling that something had eluded them.'

Much of the subsequent literature on the Rose effect can be thought as a search for that elusive something. Before reviewing the 'Rose vine' that has grown from Rose's roots, it is critical to have an idea of the currency unions that this literature investigated. As shall become clear, the type of currency union that the pre-euro literature investigated is extremely different to that of the euro area.

Pre-euro area currency unions

Rose (2000a) lists all the currency unions (CU) and CU-like monetary arrangements from 1970 onwards. This is reproduced in Table 2.1. There are three types of CU in his table. The first two columns show the hub-and-spoke CU arrangements. As Figure 2.1 shows with a schematic diagram for the USA, hub and spoke CUs involve small nations (the spokes) adopting the currency of their dominant trade partner (the hub). The hubs are the USA, France, Britain, Australia and New Zealand.

There are two types of bilateral trade flows in hub and spoke arrangements: flows between the hub and a spoke and flows between the spokes. Most hub-spoke trade flows involve the exchange of extremely different goods (so-called Heckscher-Ohlin trade). For example, the USA sells machinery to Barbados while Barbados sells rum to the USA. The spoke-spoke flows are typically very small, as is true of trade among most poor nations.

The third column of the table lists the second type of CU, namely multilateral currency unions. The two major multilateral currency unions that existed before the euro are the West African CFA arrangement and the Caribbean arrangement, the ECCA. These CUs are among nations that are tiny economically by world standards. The fourth column lists a series of highly idiosyncratic CU pairs often involving a very local hegemony, like Switzerland and Liechtenstein, or Italy and San Marino. Rose (2000a) does not have data for all these; I have put asterisks against the ones that are included in his study.

Another way to look at the oddness of the non-European currency union pairs is to plot their openness ratios. The openness ratio is just the sum of trade divided by real GDP, where the trade is the bilateral trade data from Rose (2000a) summed across all of each nation's trade partners. The results are displayed in Figure 2.2. The top panel shows all 141 nations with data. The bottom panel includes only nations that have openness ratios of less than 200% of GDP.

The top panel shows that there are some extremely open nations that also share a currency with some other nation.[6] These nations' openness is so unusual that it is hard to see what is going on with the rest. There are six nations with openness above 200%: Bahamas (1400%), Singapore (750%), Liberia (600%), Bahrain (400%), Kiribati (370%) and Belgium-Luxembourg (320%). All but one of these is involved in a currency union. Eyeballing the list, it is clear that many of these are centres of transit trade. (For example, due to Singapore's excellent port, shipping services, and lack of corruption, many East Asian exports to the USA and Europe are transhipped via Singapore.) The bottom panel excludes these extremely open nations so as to better see the others.

Table 2.1 The Rose garden, currency unions considered in Rose (2000a)

Hub and spoke arrangements		Multilateral currency unions	Misc.
*Australia	*USA	CFA	*India
Christmas Island	American Samoa	*Benin	*Bhutan
Cocos (Keeling) Islands	Guam	*Burkina Faso	*Denmark
Norfolk Island	*US Virgin Islands	*Cameroon	Faeroe Islands
*Kiribati	Puerto Rico	*Central African Republic	*Greenland
*Nauru	Northern Mariana Islands	*Chad	Turkey
*Tuvalu	*British Virgin Islands	Comoros	N. Cyprus
Tonga (pre '75)	*Turks & Caicos	*Congo	Singapore
*France	*Bahamas	*Cote d'Ivoire	Brunei
*French Guyana (OD)	Bermuda	Equatorial Guinea (post '84)	Norway
*French Polynesia	*Liberia	*Gabon	Svalbard
*Guadeloupe (OD)	Marshall Islands	Guinea-Bissau	South Africa
Martinique (OD)	Micronesia	*Mali (post '84)	Lesotho
Mayotte	Palau	*Niger	Namibia
*New Caledonia (OT0)	*Panama	*Senegal	Swaziland
*Reunion (OD)	*Barbados	*Togo	Switzerland
Andorra	*Belize	ECCA	Liechtenstein
*St.Pierre & Miquelon	*Britain	*Anguilla	Spain
Wallis & Futuna Islands	*Falkland Islands	*Antigua and Barbuda	Andorra
Monaco	*Gibraltar	*Dominica	Singapore
*New Zealand	Guernsey	*Grenada	Brunei
*Cook Islands	Jersey	*Montserrat	Italy
*Niue	Isle of Man	*St Kitts and Nevis	San Marino
Pitcairn Islands	*Saint Helena	*St Lucia	Vatican
Tokelau	Scotland	*StVincent	Morocco
	*Ireland (pre '79)		Western Sahara

Notes: This lists all the pre-euro area currency unions and CU-like monetary arrangements from 1970 onwards.
*Indicates that the nation is included in the sample of Rose (2000a).
Source: Rose (2000a) appendix table and footnotes.

Since income is on the horizontal axis, it is easy to identify nations in the hub-and-spoke currency arrangements. Hubs are always rich and spokes are usually poor, so the spokes are the circles to the left and the hubs are the circles to the right. The nine rich nations participating in CUs are (by declining order of GDP per capita): USA, Bermuda, Australia, Norway, France, Denmark, New Zealand, Italy and UK. Note that Rose (2000a) does not use data for all of these. For example, Bermuda, Denmark, Italy and Norway have no trade data with their CU partners so they are not included.

Given simple combinatorics, there are many, many more spoke-spoke pairs than hub-spoke pairs (e.g. Rose (2000a) lists 16 nations using the US dollar, which implies $16^2/2 = 128$ spoke-spoke bilateral flows and 16 hub-spoke flows). Thus most of the CU pairs in the data will be between the nations with circles in the left part of the bottom panel.

Figure 2.2 CU nations tend to be very small, poor and open

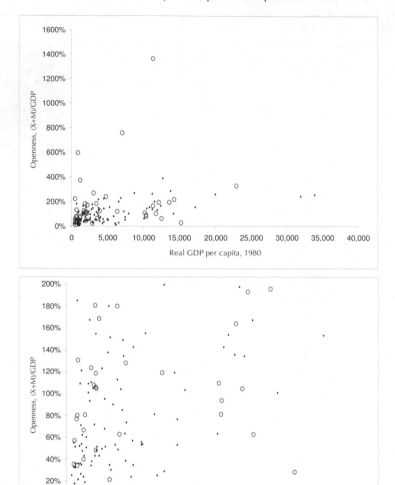

Notes: Real GDP per capita on horizontal axis (US$); total trade to real GDP on vertical axis (%).
Source: My calculations on the Rose (2000a) data for 1980.

The main point of these graphics is that nations involved in currency unions are a long way from average nations. The income levels of currency union members are either noticeably higher than the average nation (the hubs) or considerably lower than the average nation (the spokes).

2.1.2   Garden pests: biases in gravity model estimations

> Without theory, practice is but routine born of habit. (Louis Pasteur)

Rose (2000a) employed a naïve version of the gravity model for his preferred specification, a version that had been widely used by policy analysts in the 1980s and

1990s (including by me in my 1994 book on Eastern EU enlargement). The inspiration for the gravity model comes from physics where the law of gravity states that the force of gravity between two objects is proportional to the product of the masses of the two objects divided by the square of the distance between them. In symbols:

$$\frac{force\ of}{gravity} = G\frac{M_1 M_2}{(dist_{12})^2};$$

In trade, we replace the force of gravity with the value of bilateral trade and the masses M_1 and M_2 with the trade partners' GDPs (in physics G is the gravitational constant).

Strange as it may seem, this fits the data very well. Yet despite its goodness-of-fit, the naïve version results in severely biased results. These biases are responsible for Rose's famous, and famously wrong, finding that a common currency is wildly pro-trade. To see this point we need to work through a bit of theory. Although the theory does involve a small number of equations, the work is handsomely rewarded. It helps us understand all the mistakes in Rose (2000a) and the subsequent literature, and why only a handful of the hundreds of estimates of the Rose effect are worth paying attention to for policy purposes. In any case, who ever said empirical-based policy analysis should be a bed of roses?

The theory behind the gravity equation[7]

The gravity model is based on an expenditure equation. The value of exports of a single good from the 'origin' nation to the 'destination' nation depends upon the good's expenditure share and the destination nation's total expenditure on tradable goods:

$$p_{od} x_{od} \equiv share_{od} E_d$$

where x_{od} is the quantity of bilateral exports of a single variety from nation o to nation 'd' (o for 'origin' and d for 'destination'), p_{od} is the price of the good inside the importing nation measured in terms of the numeraire, so $p_{od} x_{od}$ is the value of the trade flow measured in terms of the numeraire. Also, E_d is the destination nation's expenditure on goods that compete with imports, i.e. tradable goods; shareod is the share of expenditure in nation-d, one a typical variety made in nation-o.

The expenditure share depends upon relative prices and the demand elasticity. A standard formulation for the relationship between the share and the relative price is:

$$share_{od} \equiv \left(relative\ price_{od}\right)^{1-elasticity}, \qquad relative\ price_{od} = \frac{p_{od}}{P_d}$$

where P_d is an index of the prices in nation-d of goods that compete with imports.

We are interested in total exports from the origin nation to the destination nation, so we have to multiply by the number of goods nation-o sends to nation-d to get the total value of bilateral exports from nation-o to nation-d. Doing this and rearranging a bit, we get:

$$V_{od} = n_o \left(p_{od}\right)^{1-elasticity} \frac{E_d}{P_d^{\,1-elasticity}};$$

where n_o is the number of goods nation-o exports to nation-d. If one takes nation-d's GDP as a proxy for its expenditure on traded goods and one supposes that the price of goods from nation-o to nation-d depends upon the distance between the two nations, this expenditure equation is very close to the gravity model. The only thing that is missing is the GDP of the exporting nation.

The data tell us that the exporting nation's GDP should be in the gravity equation, but what is the reason? The answer involves an elementary economic fact: the exporting nation must sell everything it produces. How much it can sell depends in turn upon the price of its goods and its market access, where market access depends upon bilateral trade costs and the geographic distribution of incomes across its trading partners. It is possible to work out the relationship precisely with a few lines of algebra. Doing so and plugging the result into the above expression for V_{od}, we have:[8]

$$V_{od} = \left(\tau_{od}\right)^{1-elasticity} \frac{Y_o}{\Omega_o} \frac{E_d}{P_d^{\,1-elasticity}};$$

where Ω_o is a measure of nation-o's market access (capital omega is a mnemonic for 'openness' to the origin nation's exports) and τ_{od} is a measure of the bilateral trade costs between nation-o and nation-d.

Taking the GDP of nation-o as a proxy for its production of traded goods, and nation-d's GDP as a proxy for its expenditure on traded goods, this can be rewritten to look just like the law of gravity.

$$\frac{bilateral}{trade} = G\frac{Y_1 Y_2}{\left(dist_{12}\right)^{elasticy-1}}; \qquad G \equiv \frac{1}{\Omega_o}\frac{1}{P_d^{\,1-elasticity}} \qquad (1)$$

where the Ys are the nations' GDPs; I have made the temporary assumption that bilateral trade costs depend only upon bilateral distance in order to make the economic gravity equation resemble the physical one as closely as possible. Importantly, G here is not a constant as it is in the physical world; it is a variable that includes all the bilateral trade costs between nations o and d, so it will be different for every pair of trade partners.

Biases in Rose (2000a)

Simplifying for clarity's sake, Rose's (2000a) preferred regression is:

$$\frac{V_{od}}{P_{USA}} = \tau_{od}^{\,1-\sigma}\left(\frac{Y_o}{P_o}\right)\frac{Y_d}{P_d}; \qquad \tau_{od} = f(dist_{od}, other\ stuff) \qquad (2)$$

In words, he deflates the bilateral trade value with the United States' CPI index, and uses real GDP, namely the national GDPs deflated by a price index that converts them to US dollars and adjusts for national price differences. Rose follows a long tradition of modelling τ as depending upon natural barriers (bilateral distance, adjacency, land border, etc), various measures of manmade trade costs (free trade agreements, etc), and cultural barriers (common language, religion, etc). His original contribution was to add a common currency dummy to the list – hard to imagine that no one had thought of it before 2000, but that's always the case with truly brilliant research.[9] Rose (2000a) estimates this on various cross-sections of his data as well as the full panel.

What is wrong with this? One big problem – the gold-medal of classic gravity model mistakes – and one small problem – the bronze-medal winner in the mistake race. The big problem is that the omitted terms – what we called the gravitational constant G in formula (1) – are correlated with the trade-cost term, since τ_{od} enters Ω_o and P_d directly (the bilateral trade costs affect the price of traded goods in nation-d and the market access of nation-o).

Where does the bias come from? Roughly speaking, the determinants of bilateral trade cost that are included in the regression have to do the work of the determinants that are left out, namely G, so the regression tells us that they are more important to trade than they really are – that's elementary econometrics (omitted variable bias). In the case at hand, the Rose (2000a) regressions tell us that currency unions matter much more than they really do.

The small problem – the bronze-medal mistake – is the inappropriate deflation of nominal trade values by the US aggregate price index. Rose (2000a) and other papers reviewed below offset this error by including time dummies. Since every bilateral trade flow is divided by the same price index, a time dummy corrects the mistaken deflation procedure.[10]

There is another serious error in Rose (2000a) and most subsequent papers. Fortunately, this one is easier to understand.

More thorns: the silver-medal of gravity mistakes

What Rose (2000a) estimates is a bit more complex than what we showed in (2). Following standard practice, he does not work with the exports from nation-o to nation-d but rather takes the average of bilateral trade. For example, he uses the average of French exports to Germany and German exports to France. There is nothing intrinsically wrong with this, but since it was done without reference to theory, most researchers commit a simple, but grave error. They mistake the log of the average for the average of the logs. In other words, researchers first average the bilateral trade flows and then take logs in preparation for the regression; Rose (2000a) and almost all gravity equations are estimated in log-log form. In fact this mistake has been repeated so many times, by so many famous economists that it has earned the crown of respectability. It is even in one of the most common references for the gravity model (Chapter 5 in Feenstra, 2003).[11]

The silver-medal mistake can seriously bias the results. The sum of the logs – the right way – is approximately the log of the sums, but the approximation gets worse as the two flows summed become increasingly different.[12] In plain English, the error will not be too bad for nations that have bilaterally balanced trade, but it can be truly horrendous for nations with very unbalanced trade. In fact, unbalanced trade is a huge issue. The biggest exporters, German, Japan and the USA, for example, sell something to most nations around the world. However, many small nations sell nothing in return, at least not to all of the big-3. Thus the problem is systematically worse for North-South trade than it is for North-North trade.

To see the sorts of bias this mistake can induce, look at what the mistake does to Germany's bilateral trade data (IMF DOTS data for the year 2000). For nations with which Germany has perfect bilateral trade balance, the log of the sums is exactly equal to the sum of the logs. But when the two flows to be averaged are quite different, the approximation becomes very wrong as Figure 2.3 shows. The extreme outlier in the figure is Germany-West Bank trade. The proper measure is 1.2 in logs, while the mistaken calculation yields 2.7 in logs. The key point here is that the mistaken measure is extra large for unbalanced bilateral trade relations. I also calculated this for Germany's trade with EU15 and other OECD partners for which bilateral trade is more balanced, but still I find errors in the order of 15% even for these fairly similar nations.

Figure 2.3 Log averaging mistake for Germany, 2000, IMF DOTS data

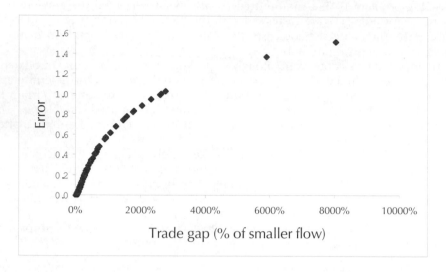

Note: The error is the incorrect (log of average) minus the correct (average of logs), for Germany's 200 or so trade partners in the IMF DOT data for the year 2000; trade gap is the absolute value of difference in bilateral exports (to and from Germany) as percent of the smaller of the two flows. The two extreme outliers are nations with extremely unbalanced trade, West Bank/Gaza Strip and Niger. The incorrect averaging makes Germany-Niger bilateral trade about 150% higher than it actually is when averaged correctly.

By the way, the error always makes the bilateral trade look bigger (Jensen's inequality), so if trade between currency union partners is systematically unbalanced, the silver-medal mistake means that the Rose effect will be systematically overestimated.

The difference between theory and practice

For the purposes of this book, the silver-medal mistake only matters if the error is especially bad for currency unions. To look at this quickly, I calculated the bilateral imbalance for all the hub and spoke CU pairs around the US dollar. I used IMF DOTS data for 2000, so not all of the islands in the Rose (2000a) list are present. Table 2.2 shows that most of the spoke-spoke trade flows are zero and the non-zero entries all have imbalances in the order of 100%, so the trade flow will be severely upward biased. The hub-spoke flows are less likely to be zero, and the trade imbalances are less severe, but in most cases they are over 50% and so also severely overestimated due to the silver medal mistake. Indeed, only one of the ten non-zero pairs has less than a 50% imbalance.

Summing up on Rose (2000)

Rose (2000a) is a great, path-breaking paper. This section has explained why the pooled estimates in Rose (2000a) – the most famous of which is the +200% estimate – should be ignored for policy purposes. They are based on an estimation technique that has subsequently been proved to be wrong by several authors, including Andy Rose himself as we shall see below. Rose (2000a) is a landmark to academics, but it should be ignored by policy makers.

Thinking of the Rose effect literature as a climbing rose springing from the Rose (2000a) roots, I turn now to the first of the three main branches of the 'Rose vine.'

Table 2.2 **Bilateral imbalance as percentage of one-way flow, US dollar currency pairs**

	Am. Samoa	Bahamas	Belize	Bermuda	Guam	Liberia	Palau	Panama	USA
Am. Samoa	–	–	–	–	–	–	–	–	–
Bahamas	–	–	–	–	–	–	–	–	–
Belize	–	-1420%	–	–	–	–	–	–	–
Bermuda	–	-120%	–	–	–	–	–	–	–
Guam	–	–	–	–	–	–	–	–	–
Liberia	–	100%	–	–	–	–	–	–	–
Palau	–	–	–	–	–	–	–	–	–
Panama	–	100%	89%	–	–	–	–	–	–
USA	–	76%	52%	91%	–	12%	–	78%	–

Source: My calculations on IMF DOTS for year 2000, export data.

2.1.3   Rose branch #1: Rose and van Wincoop (2001)

> I pass with relief from the tossing sea of Cause and Theory to the firm ground of
> Result and Fact. (Winston Churchill)

Once the gold-medal mistake became clear when Jim Anderson and Eric van
Wincoop published an influential paper in the *American Economic Review* (Anderson
and van Wincoop, 2001), Andy Rose immediately teamed up with Eric van Wincoop
to try to correct it. Rose and van Wincoop (2001) was the result and it shows that the
gold-medal error leads to a severe upward bias in the Rose effect.

Rose and van Wincoop address the model mis-specification issue in two ways. The
simplest is to include origin-nation and destination-nation dummies in a cross section regression. With these country dummies, the estimated Rose effect is radically
lowered; it falls by 2.7 standard deviations. However, this diminished Rose effect is
still mighty; without the country dummies a common currency is estimated to boost
trade by 3.97 times; with them by 2.48 times.

A mistaken correction of the mistake

Putting in time-invariant country-specific fixed effects is wrong, as the simple theory
laid out above shows clearly. The omitted terms in the 'gravitational constant' G
reflect factors that vary every year, so the country dummies need to be time varying.
If the researcher forgets about this and includes time-invariant country dummies, as
Rose and van Wincoop did, part of the bias may be eliminated. But since there will
be a time varying residual in the error, the results will still be biased to the extent that
trade costs are also time varying. This problem may be relatively minor in the Rose-
VanWincoop data since there is very little time variation in the CU dummy (more on
this below).

This point probably explains why the second, harder way of correcting for the relative-prices-matter effect in Rose-van Wincoop yields such a different result. Given all
the structure imposed on the demand system – I mean the gravity equation – the
econometrician can actually generate data for the omitted variables, what was called
the 'gravitational constant' above. When they do, the estimated Rose effect is again
radically reduced. Doing some rough calculations on the numbers in the paper suggests that the coefficient on the common currency dummy falls to 0.65, or about one
more standard deviation; with this the estimated Rose effect is 91%.

Lessons: still a rosy scenario

What are the lessons?

(1) The estimates in the preferred regression in Rose (2000a) are just plain wrong. They are overestimated. They are overestimated because the naïve gravity model is mis-specified and this mis-specification matters hugely in the dataset of Rose (2000a).[13]

History divides neatly into two parts: pre Rose-van Wincoop and post Rose-van Wincoop. Pre-Rose-van Wincoop, we believed the 200% currency-union effect might have been correct. Post-Rose-van Wincoop, we know better. More generally, one should never pay attention to estimates of the Rose effect that come from the naïve gravity model, i.e. one without fixed effects à la Anderson and van Wincoop or an equivalent correction (see below).

(2) The Rose effect was still blooming after this correction; the best estimate is that it boosts trade by 1.9 times.

(3) The omitted variable bias (stemming from G) is still in the Rose-van Wincoop numbers, so they are still too high.

2.1.4   Rose branch #2: omitted variables

If there were such a thing as the 'Gravity model for fun and profit handbook', page 1 would give this advice: 'To amaze your friends with another important trade effect, develop a new proxy for trade costs and use a really big dataset; success is not guaranteed, but you're likely to find significance (standard errors involve the inverse of the square root of number of observations) and you'll have loads of fun in any case.' This is too cynical, but the basic point is that the gravity model omits an incredible range of factors that are likely to affect bilateral trade – I've seen people get statistically significant coefficients on time zones, language proximity, membership in the Austro-Hungarian Empire, presence of a Chinatown in the two capitals just to name a few. More to the point, consider the trade among the nations listed in Table 2.1 and ask yourself: 'Can we be sure that Rose has not left out some key trade-boosting factor that operates between many CU pairs?'

This matters for the Rose effect estimate since many of those omitted factors may be correlated with the CU dummy. As mentioned above, this leads to an omitted variable bias that implies that the reported effect is too large. There are ways of addressing this problem econometrically, and we'll get to them soon. It is useful, however, to get an idea of just what sort of omitted variables we are talking about.

Exceptions that prove the Rose[14]

When the editors of *Economic Policy* at the presentation of the original Rose paper said they had 'an uneasy feeling that something had eluded them', one of the many things that bothered them was that they did not know enough about the particulars of the CU pairs that drove Rose's results. Maybe if one were an expert on West African trade, as one panellist suggested to me, one would have known exactly what omitted variable explained the overestimate of the Rose effect. The literature follows up on this in two ways. The first is to look at particular cases where we do really understand what was going on. The second is to play with the CU dummy. I address these approaches in order.

A parable

Imagine an economist asserted that the growth of the money supply was the main cause of long-run inflation and estimated the link using a huge international dataset. Using money supply growth and a handful of other variables that were available for 150 nations, he or she estimates that the money-price elasticity is unity and every other explanatory variable has a negligible effect on inflation. Then suppose another economist showed that Ireland's money supply grew at 300% for decades but its inflation rate was zero. This would make one pause. It would make one think that maybe something else is going on. The point is that counterexamples matter in empirical work; the counter-example investigator can consider a much more subtle model of the phenomenon since much more information is available than in the case of 150-nation sample.

I think the counter-example approach is especially important for the Rose effect. The sorts of variables that are available for 150 nations are the sorts of variables that matter for average nations. But Rose looked at a phenomenon that was limited to distinctly non-average nations. Thus, maybe using the 150 nation dataset approach guarantees that no one can find the 'silver bullet' pro-trade variable that would make the Rose effect disappear because no one bothered to gather internationally comparable information on a factor that matters only for a couple of dozen very unusual nations. This is why I think the counter examples considered below must be taken very seriously.

Revolutions, economic chaos and asymmetric inflation lead to CU dissolution

Many currency union break ups are done in the context of, or as the result of massive social, economic and/or political turmoil, many in the context of revolutions. As Thom and Walsh (2002) write:

> Many of these unions ended as part of a bloody decolonizing process followed by the adoption of Marxist/autarkic policies, bilateral trade deals with the Soviet Union or China, and a descent into economic chaos – France and Algeria, whose independence was granted only after a bitter struggle; India and Pakistan, who ended their currency union after the war of 1965; Pakistan and Bangladesh, who split up after the war of 1971; South Africa and Southern Rhodesia (Zimbabwe) who were ejected from the Commonwealth and had trade sanctions imposed as they broke with sterling; the five Portuguese colonies in Africa, that broke with Portugal after wars of liberation followed by civil wars. In all these cases and many others it is very likely that trade between the former currency union partners would have collapsed regardless of the currency regime in force.

If this is right, the silver-bullet is the mysterious third cause that drove the revolution, currency union break up and decline in trade. The same is true for currency union joiners. The decision to adopt a currency – for example, to dollarize – takes place in the context of great political and economic changes, many of which could be expected to affect trade. Plainly no one has good data on such factors – oh sure there are proxies to be found in hyperspace – but such things really cannot be accurately measured with a one-dimensional variable; if they could, we wouldn't need historians and political scientists. Be that as it may, my point is that one cannot see whether the Rose effect survives the inclusion of this sort of mysterious third effect in the Rose, Rose-Wincoop or Glick-Rose datasets. We also need case studies.

Thom and Walsh (2002): the bloom on 'my wild Irish rose' is not for the taking

Ireland used the British pound before its independence. After independence and the introduction of the Irish pound in 1927, the pound-punt exchange rate was held at 1-to-1 with no margins. Talks leading up the European Monetary System suggested that this peg would remain in the context of the ERM since everyone initially expected Britain to join. When Thatcher said no in 1979, Ireland was forced to choose between 'Europe' (as they call it in Britain) and the ERM on one hand, and Britain and sterling on the other. Ireland chose Europe and the 1-to-1 peg was abandoned. Market forces lifted the rate rapidly away from the level it had been at for 50 years. What happened to Anglo-Irish trade?

Figure 2.4 UK's share of Irish trade, 1924-98

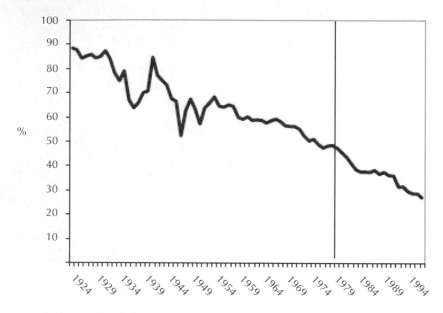

Source: (Thom and Walsh, 2002)

Since Ireland and the UK were both embedded in the EEC, the termination of the currency union did not and could not raise bilateral trade barriers. Moreover, both nations were run by stable, predictable governments and although there certainly were a number of idiosyncratic factors affecting bilateral trade, one has a very good idea of what they were and very good data that allows one to control for them. In short, we should be able to learn a lot about the Rose effect by studying the Irish case. One recent investigation of this example, Thom and Walsh (2002), finds no evidence from time series or panel regressions that the change of the exchange rate regime had a significant effect on Anglo-Irish trade. Should we be shocked?

Let's set out the priors. If the Rose effect discussed in Rose (2000a) is roughly right, the currency regime switch should have reduced Anglo-Irish trade to about a third of its initial level. The impact on Ireland should have been massive since the UK absorbed about half Ireland's exports at the time. Even if there were countervailing forces generated by the break up, it is hard to imagine any such forces that would – all else equal – raise Anglo-Irish trade by enough to substantially offset a Rose effect of -200%. By contrast, if the lower ranges of the Rose effect are right – say the effect is 15% – then we might miss the Rose effect in the Irish experience – especially if one thinks the 15% would take a number of years to be realized. My point here is that the Irish experience might help us reject a big Rose effect, but not a modest one.

Inspection of Figure 2.4 shows that the initial Rose effect just could not have been right. OK, one should run some regressions and talk about the standard errors (Thom and Walsh do), but really, would you ever believe a regression that says the data in this figure were generated by a model where trade would have dropped by 200% in 1979 were it not for some offsetting effect?[15]

I think there are other lessons in Figure 2.4.

The gradual decline of Anglo-Irish trade was due to structural changes, in my opinion – mainly changes in the Irish economy. As Ireland developed from a potato-exporting agrarian economy into the Celtic Tiger it is today, its trade pattern naturally eroded from its historical overdependence on its nearest market (the UK). This sort of thing is not in any version of the gravity model. The closest would be to allow for a separate GDP per capita variable for exporter and importer nations (for the exporter it would reflect structural shifts, for the importer an income elasticity), but Rose only includes the product of the two. Now suppose one threw into the gravity equation the 1965 Anglo-UK free trade agreement, the 1974 adhesion to the EEC and a CU dummy. Moreover, suppose one did this in a panel where it is not really possible to check for serial correlation in the errors. Plainly, the CU dummy would pick up most of the action of the omitted variables that explained Ireland's historic over dependency on the British economy. One could throw in proxies for colonial relations in various guises, but none of this would pick up the structural transformation of the Irish economy. Moreover, the history related by Thom and Walsh makes it clear that the reduced dependency on the British market – which was driven by factors that are unobservable to the gravity model – is one of the factors that caused the Currency Union to break up (more on reverse causality below).

Fidrmuc and Fidrmuc (2003): Central and Eastern European break-ups

The eyeball evidence for a large Rose effect looks much better for the recent break-ups of currency unions in Central and Eastern Europe. Figure 2.5, taken from Fidrmuc and Fidrmuc (2003), shows that the break-ups were followed by dramatic drops in bilateral trade.

The top left panel makes that best case for a large, negative Rose effect due to a currency union break-up. In 1993, Czechoslovakia went through a 'velvet divorce' just a few years after its 'velvet revolution'. The two parts of the nation separated into the Czech Republic and the Slovak Republic. They maintained a customs union (no tariffs between them and a common external tariff) until they simultaneously joined the EU's customs union. On the face of it, this is just the sort of natural experiment one should study. Figure 2.5 plots year-by-year estimates of the above normal level of trade between the partners (this is the exponent of the pair dummy, e.g. the Czech and Slovak dummy in the Czechoslovak case). But even here one must raise a note of caution. As Fidrmuc and Fidrmuc's paper concludes:

Our findings are broadly consistent with earlier findings on currency unions. In particular, Rose (2000a) shows that a common currency increases bilateral trade flows approximately three times. Indeed, we found a decline of bilateral trade intensity by about this factor during the first years of independence. However, we cannot separate the effect of the currency separation from that of the political disintegration as both effects occurred (more or less) simultaneously in the countries under scrutiny.

The total drop was less than the size of Rose's first estimate of 200%, with the size of the pair dummy falling 100% from about 4.0 to about 2.0. At one extreme, we could claim that the only thing affecting this trade was the loss of a common currency. This is rather naïve, but it gives a Rose effect of 2.0, which is similar to many estimates. Yet one suspects that political and economic disintegration also lowered trade. This means that a 100% currency union trade effect is too high; the Rose effect in isolation would be smaller. To explore this conjecture, it would be interesting to revisit the Fidrmuc-Fidrmuc data using some of the more sophisticated methods discussed above to sort out the two effects.

Figure 2.5 Trade collapses in Central and Eastern Europe

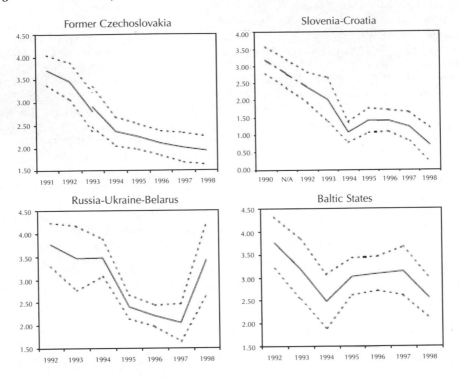

Source: Fidrmuc & Fidrmuc (2003).

Further observations follow from this work. Fidrmuc and Fidrmuc provide a qualitative discussion of the changes that accompanied the currency union dissolutions. Their discussion makes it clear that many time-varying, pair-specific omitted variables that affect trade were spawned by the same forces that lead to the CU break-up. To list just one of a dozen stories, the Czechs and Slovaks maintained free trade after the currency split, but they set up border controls that some businesses claimed acted as a trade barrier. None of these stories could be included in regressions like Rose estimates since there would be no way to gather such data for 100+ nations. The lessons from these two cases are unclear in terms of specifics, but crystal clear in terms of generalities – lots of other complicated stuff matters. And it is the sort of factors on which we will never have good, internationally comparable data. In short, gravity equations will always have omitted variables.

A recent paper takes issue with the Fidrmuc-Fidrmuc paper when it comes to the former Yugoslavia. Using more complete data than Fidrmuc and Fidrmuc (2003), De Souza and Lamotte (2006) find that the drop in trade was not dramatic but rather smooth.

Pair dummies: Glicks 'N Roses

Andy Rose was, of course, well aware of the omitted variable bias critique even before it was echoed many times by Economic Policy referees and panellists in Helsinki. He was also well aware that using pair-specific dummies would wipe out all idiosyncratic level effects between all pairs of nations. The only sticking point is that this tends to throw the roses out with the vase water. It eliminates all cross-section variation from the residual, so the identification comes solely from time series variation.[16] In plain

English, we need lots of data to do this. As he explains it, he didn't do it in Rose (2000a) since there was too little time variation in his original dataset. In Rose (2001a) he shows what this means. Using pair fixed effects on his original dataset, the Rose effect wilts (the raw estimate on the CU dummy is -0.38 and the standard error is 0.67).

Pakko and Wall (2001)

Pakko and Wall (2001) independently obtain the same results using a more general approach in terms of fixed effects and data. They use the Rose (2000a) dataset but instead of averaging the two-way bilateral flows (i.e. Germany's exports to Denmark and Denmark's exports to Germany), they preserve the uni-directional flows. This allows them to impose direction-specific pair dummies, i.e. two different dummies per bilateral flow – a technique that is more general than in Rose (2001a). Although they get Rose-like estimates of the Rose effect without pair dummies, they find that the Rose effect droops and withers away completely with pair dummies.

Rather than pushing quickly on to the next dataset and empirical technique as does Rose (2001a), Pakko and Wall take the time to crush the rose petals one-by-one. Here is how they put it:

> Independently, Rose (2001a) obtains these same results using the general fixed-effects model. However, he rejects the findings on the grounds that the statistical insignificance of the common-currency dummy is due to a small number of switches in common-currency status. While it may well be true that the statistical insignificance of the common currency dummy should not be taken to mean that the effect is not positive, this misses the point. A comparison of the two sets of results suggests that pooled cross-section estimates are not reliable because they are biased by the exclusion or mismeasurement of trading pair-specific variables. This is evident in the dramatically different coefficients on the GDP and per capita GDP variables that are found when using the two methods. In other words, the restrictions necessary to obtain the pooled cross-section specification from the fixed-effects specification are rejected, indicating that the fixed-effects specification is preferred.
>
> The difference between the two methods in their estimates of the trade-creating effect of a common currency is a separate issue. The proper conclusion to draw is that, when the statistically preferred fixed-effects specification is used, there is no statistically significant evidence of large trade effects (positive or negative). Although this means that Rose's results cannot be supported statistically, the small number of switches precludes us from saying much about the effects of common currencies on trade, although the tripling of trade found by Rose is well outside of a 95 percent confidence interval.

This is a critical point that should not be overlooked by researchers. If you can show that the pooling assumptions are false, then you should ignore all pooled estimates for policy purposes.

Rose revival

> O My Luve's like a red, red rose/ .../ And I will luve thee still, my dear/ Till a' the seas gang dry/ .../ And I will come again, my Luve,/ Tho' it were ten thousand mile.
> (Robert Burns, A Red, Red Rose)

Andy Rose is not a man to shy from a challenge. He saw the wilting of the Rose effect as a lack of data and set about collecting an enormous panel dataset. He was, so to speak, trying to graft the old flowering stem on to a healthy new dataset, and guess what? The flower continued to blossom. The massive dataset he collected included annual data from 1948 to 1997 on bilateral trade between 217 countries. Theoretically, that's $50(217^2)/2 = 2,354,450$ data points, but with missing observations and zero flows (lots of little nations sell nothing to each other), the new Rose dataset has 219,558 observations.

Glick and Rose (2002) exploit this data in a number of ways. They throw in pair-specific dummies that soak up any sort of idiosyncratic omitted variables that do not vary between 1948 and 1997. This, of course, mimics the impact of country-dummies as in Rose-van Wincoop, but it goes further. The result was, as we should have expected in the post-Rose-van Wincoop world, that the size coefficient drops dramatically – about 5 standard deviations from an estimated coefficient of 1.3 to 0.65. This brings down the Rose effect from 3.7 to 1.9 times more trade among CU pairs (both estimates are statistically significant at any conceivable level of confidence).

What is going on here? The estimates are still biased

Pretend, for a moment, that Glick and Rose did their regression in two stages. First, they regressed the left-hand side variable on the time-invariant pair dummies. Second, they regressed the residuals from that regression on the main right-hand side variables, distance, CU and the joint real GDP variable. This procedure is terribly inefficient in the econometric and practical sense, but it is very efficient from an intuitive stand point.

The first stage strips out all time-invariant features of each bilateral trade flow. This completely removes the bias stemming from the cross-section correlation between the currency union (CU) dummy and various omitted determinants of bilateral trade costs. It does the same for the cross-section correlation between what we called the gravitational constant term G and the CU dummy. However, there is almost surely a bias left. We know that the relative-prices-matter term varies over time, so there will still be a correlation with CU, after all the theory tells us that the G term contains CU and CU itself is time varying.

Second, there may still be a bias stemming from time-series correlation with omitted variables. For example, if currency union encourages nations to deepen other forms of integration that are unobservable to the econometrician, then CU and the unobserved variables could be correlated over time as well as in a cross-section sense. This is especially true since each pair gets only one dummy for the full 1948-97 data period.

Stop and smell the roses

What do we learn from this? First, the impact of allowing for country-specific idiosyncrasies (either via the Rose-Wincoop partner-dummy procedure or by the Glick-Rose technique of pair dummies) reduces the Rose effect massively. This confirms yet again that the original +200% Rose effect was overestimated. Of course, 90% more trade is still a huge number, but 200% is huger.

Second, the Glick-Rose result should have a large 'caveat emptor' stamped across its forehead. The pair dummies mean that all the identification is coming from the way in which trade between CU pairs changes over the sample, compared to the way it changes for the non-CU pairs, controlling for other factors. The Glick-Rose data have lots of pairs that leave monetary or currency unions, but very few that join (16 joiners and 130 leavers, with almost all of them having happened before the post-war independence wave ended around 1970). This means that the results are being driven by how much trade dropped after a nation leaves a monetary union, not by how much trade is created by a currency union. Nitsch (2002) estimates these effects of currency union joiners separately and finds the point estimate is small (about +8%) and statistically indistinguishable from zero.

To put it differently, if you want to know how much a small nation's trade might drop if something happens such that it has to, or wants to, leave its currency union, then the Glick-Rose numbers are what you need. If you want to know how much trade a small nation would gain from abandoning its own currency and adopting someone else's, the Glick-Rose numbers are not what you need. I think we have to admit that there just haven't been enough new currency unions to answer the question. Or at least not until the euro area came along, but I'm saving that part of the story for later.

Why are the country and pair dummy results so similar?
Third, the point estimates from the Rose-Wincoop and Glick-Rose approaches are amazingly similar. With the naïve gravity model the Rose effect is 3.97 in the Rose-Wincoop dataset; it is 3.66 in the Glick-Rose dataset. Allowing country-specific idiosyncrasies drops the estimate to 1.9 times more trade among CU pairs in both datasets.

This, I believe, is reassuring on the one hand, but worrying on the other. The reassurance is obvious; different datasets, same results. The worry is that it seems to make no difference whether one controls only for country-specific idiosyncrasies or one controls for country-specific idiosyncrasies and all other pair-specific idiosyncrasies. Why worry?

My priors are that there are omitted variables correlated with the CU dummy – e.g. the quality of FTAs, informal ethnic networks, foreign direct investment flows (trade and FDI are complements empirically), and many more – for which the data is non-existent or too poor to use in a regression. If my priors are right, the pair dummies are not doing their job properly. The why-part is easy.

Many of the pair-specific omitted variables probably varied over the five decades in the Glick-Rose dataset. Thus, putting in a time-invariant pair dummy leaves a time-series trace in the residual and this trace is probably still correlated with the CU dummy. In particular, there are probably pair-specific factors that caused nations to leave currency unions and these are probably time-varying. This is certainly the lesson to draw from the case studies. More rigorously, Nitsch (2002) uses a large panel of currency union pairs to identify factors involved in the break-up. Inter alia, he finds that departures from currency unions tend to occur when there are large inflation differences among member countries, and when there is a change in the political status of a member.[17]

Glick and Rose try out an admirable range of robustness checks, but they obviate most of the merit of the exercise by trying them one by one. For example, they use data from tiny nations in 1950 in the same regression as data from the United States in 1995. It would take a brave soul to assert that the income elasticity of imports was the same number in these two cases. Tenreyro (2001) is particularly strong on this idea that one must address all the problems together. Sure, that's a lot of regressions to try, but you have to water the thorn to harvest the rose.

2.1.5   Rose branch #3: complicated mis-specification

There are two ways of correcting for omitted variable biases. The Glick-Rose approach works by throwing lots of dummies into the regression. The alternative works by throwing lots of observations out of the regression. That sounds strange, but it has many merits. Torsten Persson's 2001 paper in Economic Policy introduced this technique into the Rose effect literature. The technique is subtle and complex; Persson explains it in technical terms (and you should have seen how technical it was before Giuseppe Bertola rewrote it in his role as Managing Editor of Persson's paper).[18]

Allow me to relate a parable that may make the nature and intractability of the problem clearer.

A parable

A few years ago, middle-age surprised a 'friend of mine' and it chose to focus on his middle; he developed a little belly. He decided to do something about it and, being an egghead, he started reading studies on the effectiveness of dieting. One study found that a week's worth of dieting was astoundingly effective. I have plotted the data in Figure 2.6 (at least the data as my friend remembers it). Crucial background: People tend to gain weight as they get older (their metabolism slows), so there is an empirical link between weight and gaining weight. A proper account of the effectiveness of dieting must take account of this. Assuming the link is linear, the study fitted the curve shown with the dashed line. However, medical science (as my friend remembers it) tells us that the true weight-to-weight-gain link is bell shaped. (Once you reach middle age you pile on an extra 10 kilos and this rapidly pushes you just beyond the normal body mass index, or BMI, range but then the process slows down.)

With this background we can see how the study overestimated the dieting effect. The solid dots are the weight gain of dieters and you can plainly see that they are below the linear dashed line. The study claimed therefore that dieting was very effective, controlling for other factors. Obviously, this is a spurious finding since the dieters' weight gain is white noise around the true-model prediction without dieting. Why the incorrect inference? The subtle interaction between nonlinearity and self-selection.

First, if the study had estimated the correct nonlinear model, it would have found that dieting was useless. Second, if the true relationship had been linear, then the deduction would have been valid. Finally, if dieting were randomly distributed across all weight classes, the model mis-specification would not have mattered since there would have been an equal number of dieters above and below the fitted line (that's what OLS does). But, dieting is self-selected. The people who are most likely to start a diet are ones, like my friend, who have just crossed into the 'jolly but not yet jelly' category.

With this parable in hand, we turn to Persson's critique.

Figure 2.6   Model mis-specification and overestimation of treatment effect

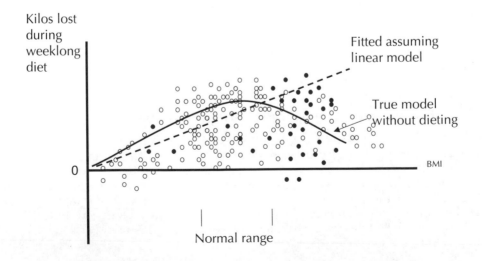

War of Roses

The Persson critique was presented in Paris at the Economic Policy Panel hosted by the Bank of France. Persson (2001) employs a matching technique that can control for this sort of nonlinearity-with-self-selection to the Rose (2000a) dataset and finds that the point estimate for the Rose effect is much lower – Persson's estimates of the Rose effect range from 1.13 to 1.66 – and they are not significant statistically. Kenen (2002) confirms part of the basic result using a different matching technique, but obtains very different results in the regression analysis.

What's going on here? It is useful to think about matching in terms of the parable. The matching technique would throw out most of the non-dieter observations since they do not match those of the dieters. If one compares the mean weight-loss of dieters and non-dieters in the narrow range just to the right of normal, there is no difference in mean, so in the case of the parable, matching would yield the correct inference. In this way, matching automatically eliminates the impact of any sort of nonlinearity by neutralizing the interaction between self-selection and nonlinearity.

What is the nature of the nonlinearity-with-self-selection in Rose's study? Persson rightly points out that while there is only one way to be linear, there are an uncountable infinity of ways to be nonlinear. One cannot check them all, but Persson thinks he may have found one important nonlinearity – a nonlinearity that concerns the openness and output link.[19] Figure 2.7 shows the suggestion.

The figure plots all residuals from Rose's preferred linear regression with the residual plotted against their corresponding log of GDP (pair product as usual). Non-CU

Figure 2.7 Persson's hypothesis for why the Rose effect is overestimated

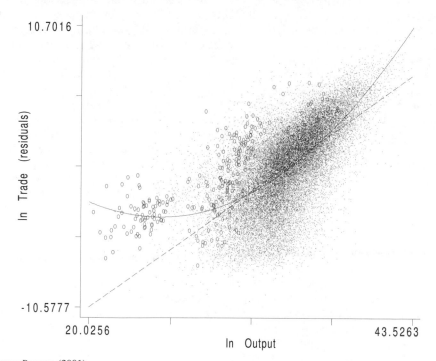

Source: Persson (2001).

observations are shown with black dots, CU observations with circles. The straight line shows the estimated linear relation between bilateral trade and output – i.e. the linear model imposed by Rose. The curved line shows the best fit allowing for a non-linear relationship between openness and output. Just as in the parable above, the non-random distribution of CU pairs teams up with the 'true' model's nonlinearity to produce an overestimation of the effect. The point is that if one compares the positions of the circles to the straight line, it looks like they have far greater trade than they should have had. If one compares them to the curved line, the circles are, on average, above the predicted relationship, but much less so than if one takes the straight line as the true model. Thus, the linear regression substantially overestimates the impact of a common currency on trade because it underestimates how much trade would have occurred without a common currency.

Persson's punch line
In short, Persson asserts that Rose (2000a) overestimated the effect since he was comparing the actual trade to a mis-specified model of what trade should have been absent from the common currency.

Further evidence comes from the fact that allowing a quadratic term in Rose's regression (i.e. pooled cross-section without country or pair dummies) drops the Rose effect estimate radically. Rose (2000a) included squared output and per-capita output terms in one of his dozens of regressions. When he did it, he found that the Rose effect drops from 3.39 times more trade to 1.95 times more; this is a four standard deviation drop in the coefficient.

Further evidence for this interpretation – albeit very indirect evidence – can be found in Glick and Rose (2002). Glick and Rose (2002) estimate the naïve gravity model on cross-section data for a handful of years reaching back to 1950. The estimated Rose effects from a selection of years are plotted in Figure 2.8. It is interesting that the size of the effect rises over time. What could this mean? One cannot know for sure, but the Persson-Kenen finding suggests a story. In 1950, many nations participated in currency unions. Most nations were still colonies and many of these used the currency of the colonizer. Or, to put it differently, the group of nations sharing common currencies was much more randomly spread. As the decade of independence arrived, many nations adopted their own currency as a symbol of sovereignty. In the Glick-Rose data there are 130 CU leavers but only 16 entries.[20] The roll-call of CU dummy pairs thinned out, but the decision to quit the colonizer's currency was surely not random. Really tiny, really open economies like New Caledonia decided they could not afford their own currency, while nations like Algeria went their own way. In this chronicle, the self-selection part of the nonlinearity-with-self-selection bias gets more severe as time passes. Thus, if you believe the Persson-Kenen account, the rising Rose effect is completely in line with your priors.

The bloom is off the rose, or is it? Rose redux

Andy Rose is not one to let a new econometric technique lay in bed till noon. When Economic Policy invited Andy to present a live rejoinder to Persson at the April 2001 Panel in Paris, he leapt to the wall with bow strung and arrow nocked. He used a new, bigger dataset and applied Persson's matching technique. Guess what? Rose (2001a) confirms that matching lowers the point estimate on the CU dummy (the Rose effect drops from 3.39 to 1.21 in the strictest match, to 1.43 in the most relaxed; that is, 21% and 43% more trade predicted for CU pairs). However, and critically, he finds that the Rose effect is statistically significant in the bigger dataset even with matching. In the end, the rose was still blooming; 20%, after all, is a pretty big number, certainly far bigger than that in the minds of most international economists in 2001.

Figure 2.8 The Rose effect over time

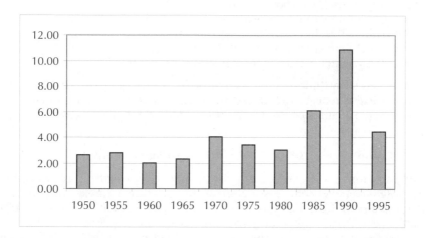

Lessons: take nonlinearity and selection seriously

Decades of gravity model research tell us that the naïve model does pretty well in most cases. The vast majority of the thousands of gravity equations estimated over the past 40 years assumed linearity without objection. But in the old days, we could not handle large datasets, so most gravity estimators used data from nations that were pretty homogeneous, like European nations plus the USA, Canada and Japan, or all Latin American nations. In these cases, linearity – even if it is wrong – is not a big deal. After all, any continuous model is approximately linear.

But the linear approximation gets worse the further one is from the point of approximation. Since estimation is, in effect, approximating the functional relationships for the average country in the sample, the problem gets worse as the sample includes more extremely large, small, open or closed nations. The problem is extra severe in the hunt for the Rose effect since nations that are members of monetary or currency unions are extremely far from average; see Figure 2.2. One way of thinking about what Persson and Kenen did is to say that they were trying to get a more homogeneous sample so that whatever nonlinear does exist is not a big deal.

I believe it is extremely important to take seriously the Persson-Kenen lesson in any gravity equation study that uses data from a very heterogeneous group of nations. The econometric theory tells us that if the true model is nonlinear, yet a linear model is estimated, then the estimated coefficients are biased if the policy under consideration is not randomly distributed across all observations. Both of these premises hold for the gravity model on the Rose (2000a), Rose and van Wincoop (2001) and Glick and Rose (2002) datasets, so we know the standard gravity-model estimate of the Rose effect is biased. To wit:

- We know that CU pairs are not random. The first-stage matching regressions confirm the suspicion raised by Table 2.1 and this has been confirmed many times over by authors such as Alesina, Barro and Tenreyro (2002), and Nitsch (2002).

- We know that the true gravity equation is nonlinear (Rose (2000a) finds a t-statistic of 24 on the GDP squared term and there may be many other nonlinearities).

Again, history bifurcates. Before the 2001 Persson-Kenen-Rose papers, we didn't think nonlinear was an issue. Now we know it is. We are not exactly sure how best to address the nonlinearity, but we know it is a problem. Two more lessons:

- For policy purposes, we should ignore all Rose effect estimates on large datasets that do not address the nonlinearity-cum-selection issue. Researchers would be wise to address it in both ways: (1) try out various nonlinearities; in the context of Rose effect regressions, be sure to try quadratic terms for GDP and GDP per capita; (2) try matching procedures like those suggested by Persson or Kenen.

- The Rose effect on multilateral data is of the order of about 20-40%, but this figure basically reflects the extent to which bilateral trade dropped between nations when a currency union pair involving a small poor nation is dissolved.

2.1.6 Rose branch #4: roster-makes-the-sun-rise reasoning

While Andy Rose was declaring 'Eureka' for having shown that a common currency bumps up bilateral trade, other researchers were declaring a Eureka for showing the reverse. Devereaux and Lane (2003), inter alia, showed that nations tend to stabilize their bilateral exchange rates against nations with whom they trade a lot, with a common currency being an extreme form of stabilization. There are many sophisticated reasons for this reverse causality ('reverse', that is, from the Rose effect perspective) but my favourite is a political economy story. If a nation's currency depreciates against its major trade partner, cheers arise from exporting firms but screams are heard from firms that import components and materials. The roles are reversed for appreciations. Since losers lobby harder[21] there is strong political pressure on a Central Bank to keep the exchange rate steady against the currency of its major trading partner, especially in very small nations where the importers and exporters dominate local politics. In extreme cases, this means adopting the major partner's currency.

The reverse causality problem is a thorn in the side of would-be Rose-effect estimators. Although one could invent elaborate stories for why the simultaneity bias might be negative, common sense tells us that the bias should lead to an upward bias. That is, at least part of the reason the circles in Persson's diagram are above the predicted trade line is because unusually open nations, especially tiny ones located near big markets, are more likely to join currency unions. In this case the conditional correlation between a common currency and trade is boosted in part by the impact of currency on trade and in part by the impact of trade on currency. This leads me to believe that all of the Rose effects discussed up to this point are too large.

Of course, this possibility occurred to Andy and in his Economic Policy article, he tries to control for this with instrumental variable techniques. His choice of instruments (inflation rates), however, was regrettable and forgettable. When he instruments for the CU dummy, the Rose effect becomes 'wildly and implausibly bigger' in Andy's own words; to wit, the Rose effect is 1.1 times 1036. To put that in context, it implies that Fiji's adoption of the Australian dollar would raise its bilateral trade to several times larger than the value of world trade. I think we can agree that his instrumental variables strategy was not successful; in fact, he abandoned the effort in subsequent papers.

Other instrumenting strategies

Three other instrumenting strategies have been mentioned in the Rose-effect literature and two have been implemented: one is based on money supplies along the lines suggested by Frankel and co-authors, and one by Tenreyro (2003). The final one, by Devereaux and Lane (2002), has not been tried to my knowledge.

Tenreyro (2003) estimates the likelihood of a nation joining a hub-and-spoke currency arrangement with the US dollar, British pound, French Franc or Australian dollar. She explains this decision using a dozen or so variables that are very closely related to right-hand side variables in the gravity equation. She finds that the probability is increasing in common language, common border, former colonial status and the smallness and poorness of the nation. The fit of this first stage regression is not very good; the pseudo-R2 is only 0.473, so roughly speaking, she only explains about half of hub-and-spoke currency pairs in her data. Since CU pairs account for less than 1% of all pairs in her data, this could be a real problem in the sense of amplifying the nonlinear-and-selection biases. Her first-stage explanatory variables are a sub-set of the second-stage explanatory variables, so the probability itself cannot be used as an instrument. To get around this, she constructs an artificial probability of any two spokes sharing the same currency by multiplying each spoke's probabilities of adopting each anchor currency and summing over the four products.

This seems a clever idea, but there are two problems. First, I would like to see what this procedure yields. For example, how well does her newly-minted fitted CU variable line up with the real CU variable? I would bet that this procedure invents lots of CU ties between very small, very open economies and thus exacerbates the Persson-Kenen problem.

Second, she writes in Alesina, Barro and Tenreyro (2002), 'The underlying assumption for the validity of this instrument is that the bilateral trade between countries i and j depends on bilateral gravity variables for i and j but not on gravity variables involving third countries.' As the simple gravity model theory laid out above shows, this identifying assumption is false. All you need to do is remember that the gravity model is essentially a demand equation and you know that each bilateral flow is affected by the trade costs of every partner of the importing nation (specifically in Equation (1), the price index P_d and every partner of the exporting nation via Ω_o). The Tenreyro identifying assumption is essentially saying that the trade between two nations depends only upon the nominal price, not the nominal price divided by an index of prices from all sources. In fact, this third country dependence is exactly what the whole Anderson-Wincoop paper is about. Curiously, she includes Anderson-Wincoop dummies in some of her regressions and thus implicitly admits that her identification strategy is based on a false premise. But maybe I missed something. Other things seem strangely upside-down in that paper; adding country dummies increases the OLS estimate of the Rose effect, in contrast to what many others have found.

In any case, she finds that instrumenting raises the Rose effect to levels that would make Andy blush as red as a rose – for example, she gets a Rose effect of 6.77 in her paper with Barro and 14.87 in her paper with Alesina and Barro (for the record, that means joining a currency union would increase a nation's trade with its CU partners by 577% and 1,387% respectively). If this is right, then Finland with its 5 million people will export more to Germany than the United States exports to the whole world; since Finland has 10 euro area partners and the effect applies to each, Finland's decision to join the euro area will double world trade – according to Tenreyro's upper estimate. Her lowest IV estimate predicts that formation of the euro area will more than double world trade.

Of course, you may think that it is inappropriate, maybe even unfair, to extrapolate from the results of small nations. But if you think that, then you don't believe the linear gravity model works well for nations that are extremely different from the average nation. In other words, you don't believe what one must believe to think the Tenreyro identification strategy makes sense.[22] Given these problems, I think we can conclude that Tenreyro's procedure failed. Probably prudent to consign it to the regrettable and forgettable bin along with Rose's instrumenting strategy.

I hasten to note that the theoretical points in Alesina, Barro and Tenreyro (2002) are interesting and useful. The empirical implementation is, in my humble opinion, a failure.

Aphides: all instruments will be bad instruments

It is hard to know exactly how it all went so wrong with the Rose and Tenreyro approaches. It helps, however, to think about the instrumenting technique. Basically, the econometrician has to invent a new data series that looks something like the CU dummy but isn't the CU dummy. This newly invented variable is thrown into the gravity model and the coefficient on the new invented variable is taken to be the currency union effect. There are several problems with this procedure:

- *Digital dummies and amplified nonlinearity-selection problems*. The CU dummy is digital by the nature of the policy under investigation. The instrument, by construction, will be a continuous variable. What this means is that the Rose effect estimate will be influenced by the sample covariance between the invented variable and the bilateral trade of all pairs. If the invented variable doesn't resemble the CU dummy very closely, it is likely to display many features that the CU dummy does not and may therefore generate an estimated coefficient that has nothing to do with the Rose effect. This point is amplified if nonlinearities are important, as I believe they are in samples that include large variations in country size. As discussed above, part of the overestimate in Rose (2000a) stemmed from self-selection and nonlinearities. The first stage of the instrumenting process guarantees non-random selection – in fact it probably makes it much worse. Just take a look at Persson's diagram and imagine what the invented variable would look like. I haven't seen the data, but my bet is that Tenreyro's invented CU variable places lots more circles (in a probabilistic sense) far above the straight line in Figure 2.7.

- *All instruments will be bad instruments*. A good instrument is correlated with the explanatory variable, but uncorrelated with the regression error. I believe all CU instruments will fail on both criteria, so no instrument is going to fit well. Having a common currency is a really unusual outcome. In reality it is governed by factors that can never be quantified in variables that exist for 150+ nations. This means a bad fit, but things are worse. No instrument will be uncorrelated with the error due to 'double omitted variables'. The first stage of fitting a currency-union model will, of course, omit many variables given the fuzzy political, social and cultural factors involved in currency choice. The instrument will not be orthogonal to these factors. Thus, if some of the variables omitted in the first-stage variables are also omitted variables in the gravity equation, then the instrument will not serve its purpose. Lots of things on which we have no reliable data could promote both CU membership and bilateral trade among CU members. Here are couple of ones that occurred to me: personal ties developed while studying in the 'hub' nation, and greater than usual mutual understanding of each other's legal systems, but the list is almost endless.

Lessons: Briar Rose

The Brothers Grimm tell the tale of a beautiful princess who came to be known as Briar Rose since she slept a hundred years in a castle surrounded by an impenetrable hedge of briars, i.e. thorns (although in my version of the tale, they are rose vines). Princes from far and wide sought to claim the great prize that lay within, but all found it impossible to get through the thorny hedge, 'for the thorns held fast together, as if they had hands, and the youths were caught in them, could not get loose again, and died a miserable death'. Then one day a particularly handsome prince came near to the thorn-hedge and 'it was nothing but large and beautiful flowers, which parted from each other of their own accord, and let him pass unhurt'.

Plainly, instrumental variable techniques are what we need to properly control for the reverse causality that must be biasing the Rose effect upwards. Maybe some day a particularly handsome instrument will show up and our problems will be solved. Up to now, however, attempts to find that every instrument have failed miserably. What might we do better? Well, surely, the idea would be to get some financial variables à la Devereaux and Lane since these may influence the CU decision without influencing bilateral trade, at least for trade data at five year intervals.

2.1.7   Meta-analysis: a rose is a rose is a rose

Readers who have made it this far may have a muddled impression of the many estimates discussed above (the main ones are summarized in Table 2.3). Wouldn't it be great to have one summary statistic, the number as it were? There is such a number but I do not believe it is useful for policy purposes.

Table 2.3 Rose effect estimates arranged by estimator

Author	OLS (pooled)		Country fixed effect time-invariant	Pair specific		Matching	
	Linear	Nonlinear	Linear	Linear	Nonlinear	Linear	Nonlinear
Rose (2000a)[a]	1.21 (0.14)		0.77 (0.16)	-0.38 (0.6)			
Rose & van Wincoop[a]	1.38 (0.19)		0.91 (0.18)				
Glick & Rose[b]	1.30 (0.13)			0.65 (0.05)	0.61 (0.05)		
Tenreyro	0.09 (0.14)						
Persson[a]		0.937; 0.69 (0.15) (0.15)				0.52 (0.320)	0.37 (0.320)
Rose response[b]				0.74 (0.052)	0.66 (0.05)	1.47-2.19 (0.09)-(0.14)	1.4 - 2.1 (0.09)-(0.14)
Pakko & Wall[a]	1.17 (0.143)			-0.378 (0.529)			
Kenen	1.7 (0.310)					1.2; 1.4 (0.30); (0.32)	

Notes: [a]Rose's five-year dataset. 1970-90. UN data. [b]Glick-Rose dataset. 1948-97. IMF data.
To find Rose effect in terms of % increase in trade, take exponent of coefficient and subtract 1.

Weighted average of all point estimates

Rose and Stanley (2004) perform a sophisticated analysis on 34 studies of the Rose effect that yield 754 point estimates. They reject the hypothesis that the true number is zero. The range they arrive at is 30% to 90%. Surely, this is taking things too literally. Or more precisely, it throws away too much information by treating all estimates as having been generated by the same process. As the authors note: 'While we have strong views about the quality of some of these estimates, each estimate is weighted equally; alternative weighting schemes might be regarded as suspect.' Please, suspect! That's what empirical researchers get paid for. All the estimates in Rose (2000a), for example, should be ignored except the difference-in-difference estimator that roughly controls for the gold-medal mistake of gravity models. Andy Rose himself showed that all of them were incorrect since the pooling assumptions necessary for them to make sense have been rejected by his papers with van Wincoop and Glick.

Moreover, the patently incorrect pooled estimates of the Rose effect – all of which are at least twice too big – are generally repeated in the literature as a way of showing that the author's dataset is sound in that it can reproduce the mistaken estimates in Rose (2000a). In other words, authors repeat them as a form of benchmarking, not for policy relevance. The meta-analysis statistical techniques are fascinating, but I don't believe they add anything to our knowledge. Deep down they are basically a weighted average of all point estimates that include many of the point estimates that have been proven to be false.

2.1.8 Lessons for the euro area from non-European experiences

I believe the cleanest estimates we have on non-European currency unions are those that use matching since these go a long way towards controlling for the omitted variable bias, and for any bias from model mis-specification. All the other estimates seem to have serious flaws that would bias them upward. On the original Rose dataset, Persson (2001) found the effect to be between 15% and 66%. Rose (2001a) found it to be between 21% and 43% on a much larger dataset. An informal meta-analysis on these four estimates would suggest a number like 30%. And we can be pretty sure that this is an overestimate since the matching procedure cannot control for reverse causality, and it seems extremely likely that the je-ne-sais-quoi factors that lead nations to adopt each other's currency also tend to promote bilateral trade.

I believe, however, that the non-European evidence has essentially zero informational content for the euro area – apart from the fact that it is worth looking for a Rose effect in Europe. The basic problem is that the non-European data are driven by nations that are very small, very poor and very open. Exactly because the currency union pairs in the data are so strange, we cannot use the 30% to predict the currency union affect for any nation that is not strange in the same way.[23] I guess this falls into the category of common sense. If you study the trade effects of a currency union on very small, very poor and very open nations, then what you learn is how much currency unions affect the trade of very small, very poor and very open nations. Did I repeat myself? Well, I guess that is why they call it common sense.

2.2 Empirical findings on the euro area

> What matters is not the length of the wand, but the magic in the stick.
> (Hagrid to Harry Potter)

Most of the Rose effect literature treats currency unions as magic wands – one touch and intra-currency-union trade flows rise between 5% and 1400%. The only question is: 'How big is the magic?' This approach was understandable when the literature was dealing with hundreds of pairs of trade among CU members. Given the amazing range of peculiar situations under study – ranging from France's trade with its overseas departments to trade between the two tiny Pacific islands Nauru and Tuvalu – one was naturally attracted by generalizations.

In Europe, however, the big-magic approach is most definitely not good enough. We know an awful lot about the affected countries, far too much to pretend that the euro will affect all their trade flows in the same way. Moreover, the euro matters far too much for easy generalizations to be appropriate. Some 290 million people use the euro, and euro monetary policy quite directly touches the lives of another 200 million people living in the non-euro area EU nations and near neighbours.

Empirical studies of the euro's trade impact [24]

Given the roaring interest sparked by Rose's papers, it was inevitable that someone would try to estimate the Rose effect for the euro area. In April 2002, Andy Rose alerted the Managing Editors of *Economic Policy* to what appears to be the first paper on the subject.[25] When I got this message, I looked up the paper and saw it was very much in the how-big-is-the-magic line – not at all what we thought the world needed, but we asked the authors to write a paper that would go much further and after some iteration, commissioned what was eventually published as Micco, Stein and Ordoñez (2003b), or MSO for short. After a massive revision of its first draft, the paper was presented to the October 2000 *Economic Policy* Panel Meeting hosted by the Bank of Greece.

The *Economic Policy* panellists were quite positive on the paper and its main conclusion that the euro had already boosted trade, but they had many questions and suggestions. In their second revision, the authors addressed almost all these concerns. After a thorough edit, MSO was published in the April 2003 issue of *Economic Policy* – an issue in which all articles dealt with the euro's impact.[26]

2.2.1 MSO (2003b)

The earliest version of MSO presented estimates of the Rose effect in the order of about 25%. These were so big that the referees and editors asked them to plot the data and see if it appeared even without conditioning for other trade-enhancing factors. The result is shown in Figure 2.9.

It is somewhat hard to see what is going on when the data are plotted from 1980 to 2002 (the latest data point MSO had), but in the right panel, the same data are plotted from 1993 to 2002. Note that there was a major change in the way the EU collected its trade data from 1993, so it is difficult to compare pre- and post-1993 figures. (Much more on this below.) In the right panel, there does indeed seem to be some sort of break in the data. But again, it is not that the touch of the euro's magic wand made trade jump up by 25%. What happened was that the euro area's trade with everyone fell – as did trade among other developing nations at the time – but the intra-euro area trade fell by less. Gomes et al. (2004) show a very similar graph, adding the data for 2003, and find similar results. Flam and Nordström (2003) plot more detailed data, showing the euro area's exports to other nations (eight other OECD nations) separately from the other-eight's exports to the euro area. The results in Figure 2.10 confirm the basic message but rely solely on export data.

The time-series are suggestive, but since bilateral trade is influenced by many things that vary over time, especially incomes, MSO estimate a gravity model on data from 1992 to 2002 for two samples, one that is quite homogeneous (only the 15 EU nations) and one with 22 developed countries that is less so.

Rose effect estimates for the euro area, 6% more trade

The cleanest results in the MSO paper are estimates done with pair fixed effects on the EU15 sample for the 1992 to 2002 period. Using this technique, MSO find that the Rose effect induced 6% more trade among euro area members.[27] This estimation

Figure 2.9 Intra-euro area trade, euro area trade with others, and trade among others, 1980-2002

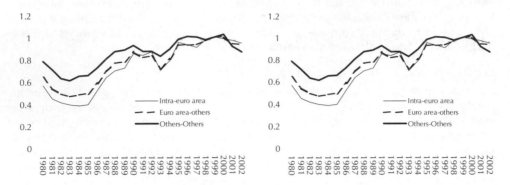

Source: MSO (2003) with some re-calculations by me (100=1999).

Notes: The series (1997=100) show the trade evolution between classified country pairs. Specifically, for every country in the sample, we calculate a trade index with euro area (EA) countries and one with non-EA countries. The EA-EA series is the unweighted average of the EA country's EA trade indices. The non-EA-non-EA series is the unweighted average of the non-EA country's non-EA trade indices. The EA-non-EA series is the average of all 'cross group' indices. Nations in the sample: Australia, Austria, Belgium-Luxembourg, Canada, Denmark, Finland, France, Germany, Greece, Iceland, Ireland, Italy, Japan, New Zealand, Netherlands, Norway, Portugal, Spain, Sweden, Switzerland, Britain, and the United States.

Figure 2.10 Intra- and extra-euro area trade, 1989 to 2002

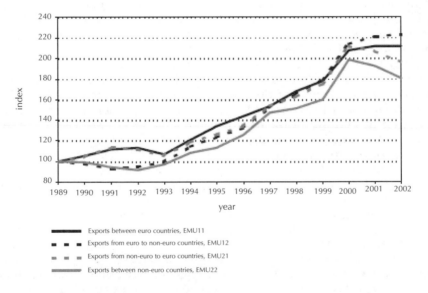

Source: Flam and Nordstrom (2003)

strategy can be thought of as a difference-in-differences estimate. Using terminology that comes from medical studies, one group of trade pairs gets 'treated', while the control group of pairs gets a placebo; here, the treatment is euro area membership and the placebo is non-membership. Using the gravity model to control for observable differences between the control group and the treatment group, the estimate tells us how much bilateral trade rose in the 'treatment' group relative to the rise in the 'control' group. This is called difference in differences, since it compares the before-and-after difference for the treatment group to the before-and-after difference for the control group.

In doing this sort of exercise, it is important to get a control group that is as comparable as possible to the treatment group as far as unobservable factors are concerned (any observable factors can be controlled for via regression analysis). Given that EU membership is an extremely complex thing – one that involves literally thousands of laws, regulations and practices that affect trade within the EU and with third nations, most of which are unobservable to the econometrician – limiting the control group to EU members is very useful.[28] Moreover, limiting the data to post-1992 data is useful since the EU changed the way it collected trade statistics in 1993.[29]

The difference-in-difference estimator on the EU sample takes seriously the lessons of Persson-Kenen (use a sample where the treatment and control groups are as homogeneous as possible), and the lessons of Anderson-van Wincoop (control for omitted variables and model mis-specification with dummies).[30] Finally, the intra-EU trade data, but especially the intra-euro area trade data, may have some serious measurement problems – intra-EU imports are under-reported due to VAT fraud.

What does this difference-in-differences technique not control for? Probably the main thing is differences between euro area and non-euro area members' implementation of EU-wide reform. The EU is continuously 'deepening' its integration, removing various barriers to the free movement of goods, people, capital and services. All EU members must adopt these measures, but many EU members delay – sometimes for years – and so the Single Market is not really a single market at any given moment. If the delays are systematically more important for the 'outs', i.e. non-euro area members than they are for the 'ins', then the euro area dummy may be biased upwards. In fact, the fastest implementers include all three of the outs (Britain, Denmark and Sweden) while the three laggards (Italy, Portugal and Ireland) are 'ins', so the MSO 6% may be biased.[31] (Much more on this point in Chapter 3.)

Estimates with other control groups

MSO also perform the difference-in-differences technique using a broader sample that includes eight extra rich nations (Iceland, Norway, Switzerland, Australia, Canada, Japan, New Zealand and the USA). Trying to control for other forms of EU integration with dummies and proxies, they find the Rose effect is 4% or 5%. This result is likely to be subject to more biases than the EU sample since many omitted factors affect trade with and among these extra nations. Just to take one example, the USA-Mexico free trade agreement (in the guise of NAFTA) was phased in slowly during the MSO period. Classical trade theory tells us that this preferential liberalization should have reduced all third nation exports to the USA and Canada. If NAFTA were a one-time thing, the pair dummies would control for this, but NAFTA was phased in slowly, so the trade-diversion effect is not fully controlled for. This matters since all non-euro area flows are used to establish a basis for what intra-euro area trade would have been were it not for the monetary union. Similarly, New Zealand and Austria deepened their trade ties during this period and the EU signed many free trade deals with third nations – some of which were shadowed by Iceland, Norway and Switzerland, but not the others. Given this, it is easy to see why limiting the sample to the EU is a useful way to control for an abundance of unobserved factors.

Biased estimates and exchange rates

For comparison with the early literature, MSO estimate the Rose effect without country or pair dummies, i.e. the commit the gold-medal error. As expected, they get a bigger estimate, about 28%, but in the post-Rose-van Wincoop world, we know that we should ignore such estimates for policy purposes.[32] The authors also do the regressions including real exchange rate variables between the US dollar and the origin nation, and the US dollar and the destination nation. The inclusion of exchange rate variables is fairly rare in gravity equations. MSO justify it on the basis of a 'valuation bias'.[33] Their specification seems quite wrong to me – I'll explain in depth when discussing the Flam-Nordström paper below – but in any case, it doesn't make much difference even though these variables turn up as highly significant. My guess is that the statistical significance of these variables arises from a correlation between their real exchange rate variables and the time residual for the relative-prices-matter term.[34]

Trade diversion?

The simplest stories behind the Rose effect are that they reduce bilateral trade costs – transaction costs are a standard suspect. If this is the case, then the euro's introduction is like a discriminatory trade liberalization among euro area members and this should lead to supply switching from non-euro area to euro area suppliers. Thus, if the simple transaction cost story is correct, all other bilateral trade flows should be reduced by anything that boosts intra-euro area trade.

MSO look for trade diversion by including a dummy that switches on when either partner is in the euro area in addition to the standard currency union dummy. They call this the EMU1 dummy, but it should have been called the EA1 dummy (see footnote 27). In any case, they find no evidence of trade diversion. Indeed, in the developed country sample, they estimate a positive impact on the euro area's trade with the rest of the world. On the EU sample, the point estimate is bigger, but it is not significantly different from zero. Moreover, the Rose effect jumps up somewhat from 4% to 13% in the big sample and from 6% to 9% in the EU sample. Alho (2002) confirms the basic finding of no trade diversion and a positive Rose effect.

Why does the Rose effect rise when they include a dummy for trade between euro area nations and third nations? Recalling the difference-in-differences interpretation, we know that the size of the Rose effect depends on what happened to intra-euro area trade compared to what would have happened without the euros. By including their EA1 dummy, they essentially take trade among non-euro area nations as their control group, instead of all non-intra-euro area trade flows. Since MSO do not properly control for free trade agreements among the third nations (e.g. they lump NAFTA, ANZCER, and EER all together in one dummy called FTA), it is difficult to know what is really happening. It would be useful to redo the MSO with more attention paid to time-varying trade arrangements among third nations.

Timing is everything

MSO also study the timing of the Rose effect. What they do is interact the CU dummy with year dummies, so they can estimate the Rose effect year by year. Of course, this means they identify the Rose effect off the cross-section variation – and we know this yields estimates that are too high due to the 'gold-medal' mistake discussed above – but it is nonetheless instructive to look at what they find. The Rose effect first appears in 1998 and increases with the introduction of notes in 2001. Finally, they use dynamic panel techniques and find the short-run Rose effect is 9% to 12%, with the long-run effect ranging from 21% to 34%.

Although it is useful to see the dynamic panel technique, the actual numbers should be ignored as far as policy is concerned. We know from the Melitz-Levy-Yeyati results that the trade effects of monetary union (what happened in 1999) may be very different than the trade effects of currency union (what happened in 2002). The dynamic panel technique, however, views them as the same so the deepening of integration that came with physical euros is confounded with the delayed effect of the monetary union. The dynamic panel technique won't tell us anything sensible until we have at least a few years of post-2002 data.

2.2.2   Berger and Nitsch (2005)

MSO (2003b) and Rose (2000a) are seminal works; they used the best available data and econometrics to investigate an important policy-relevant issue. Even if subsequent data show that all their conclusions were wrong, they will remain great papers.

To many economists, the MSO paper was important in that it raised the possibility that a Rose effect was happening in Europe's monetary union. What was particularly striking was that they found an effect on just four years of data. The fact that the size of the effect was small just made their findings more believable. MSO, however, was never going to be the final word – we just cannot get a reasonable estimate of the euro's trade effect with just four years of data.

MSO became an instant target for the shrink-the-Rose-effect brigade, and the brigade's informal captain – Volker Nitsch – was in the lead. Berger and Nitsch noted four crazy things in MSO's findings, or as they put it politely, things that 'invite further study':

(1) The trade effect of the euro is too large relative to the trade effect of EU membership. Their findings imply that the adoption of the euro has, in four years, had almost the same impact as the radical liberalization of the Single Market Programme that has been gradually phased in since 1986, with much of it completed by 1992. Anyone who follows European integration knows this is just crazy.

(2) Trade among EMU members seems to jump up in 1998, i.e. one year before the euro's launch as an electronic currency. Indeed, the Rose effect estimate seems to climb gradually over MSO's data period and this suggests that maybe something other than the euro was affecting intra-euro area trade. More to the point, it suggests that MSO may be having trouble sorting out the effects of monetary integration among euro area nations and non-monetary integration.

(3) The size of the Rose effect is quite sensitive to disaggregation by country. MSO find that the euro had the largest trade effect for DM-bloc countries, but it is negative for Greece and Portugal (although only significantly so for Greece). It is positive but insignificantly different from zero for Finland. This means the 'magic wand' is not working correctly for 4 of the 11 euro area members (Belgium and Luxembourg are treated as one).

(4) When the DM bloc is dropped from the sample, the Rose effect disappears. This seems strange since – again referring to medical statistics – the dosage effect is all wrong (in showing that a drug helps, medical studies try to establish that the size of the benefit is sensitive to dosage as evidence that the result is not due to unobservable characteristics of the patient). The euro was a far, far bigger policy change for Greece than it was for Germany, yet Germany seems to get a significant positive Rose effect while Greece gets a significant negative effect whose magnitude is almost twice that of Germany's.

Shifting from critique to contribution, Berger and Nitsch add a fifth year of data (namely 2003), and re-estimate MSO using recently revised trade data. Interestingly, both the data revision and extra year seem to greatly increase the Rose effect. (Below, I'll argue that this is a sign that, as Marcellus said so eloquently when Hamlet slipped off for a tête-à-tête with a ghost, 'Something is rotten in the state of Denmark'.)

They also put the adoption of the euro in historical perspective, viewing the euro area as 'a continuation, or culmination, of a series of policy changes that have led over the last five decades to greater economic integration among the countries that now constitute the [euro area]'. Specifically, they use data for MSO's developed country sample of the EU15 plus eight reaching back to 1948! Their bottom line is that throwing in a time-trend-dummy for trade among the 11 euro area members wipes out the Rose effect completely. There is surely something to the euro area-as-a-continuum idea – see Mongelli, Dorrucci and Agur (2005) for a more elaborate formalization of the idea that European trade and policy integration are a dialectic process – and this surely makes it hard to separate the Rose effect from the effects of other integration initiatives. However, I think it is too blunt to throw in a time trend for the euro area 12. European integration has affected all EU members equally. In future drafts, I hope the authors will repeat more of the MSO robustness checks with their updated data, and redo the time trend exercise, but with a trend for EU membership as a whole. It would also be interesting to see if they could develop a data-based index of extraordinarily close integration among the DM bloc, rather than the EA12. For example, one might take estimates of bilateral pass-through elasticities as proxies for pair-specific trade integration, the notion being that pass through would be bigger between more tightly integrated partners.[35]

2.2.3   Flam and Nordström (2003)

This is probably the best paper in the field to date. It avoids the gold, silver and bronze medal mistakes that plague the rest of the papers in this literature. Moreover, they use a dataset that probably has far fewer data issues than those used by MSO and their followers, namely they use bilateral exports rather than an average of bilateral exports and imports. The use of direction-specific bilateral trade flows is what the basic gravity theory suggests should be used. Moreover, it allows them to look at an issue that concerns all the non-euro area nations, whether the euro puts their exporters at a disadvantage in the euro area. Additionally, they also alert the reader to the problems with European trade data collection (much more on this below). Finally, they perform their regressions on sector data as well as aggregate data.

Their basic findings on the aggregate data are in line with MSO, both in terms of size and timing. Their preferred estimate uses the three non-euro area and eight extra rich nations as the control group and they find the Rose effect implies about 15% higher trade; euro area trade with other nations (in either direction) is boosted by about half that. When they use the cleanest definition of the control group – other EU nations – the Rose effect is only 9%. Their findings on the sectoral data suggest that the Rose effect is only present in sectors marked by differentiated products, confirming the earlier results of Taglioni (2002), and Baldwin, Skudelny and Taglioni (2005).

There are a few puzzling findings in Flam-Nordström. As in MSO, they find that the Single Market has about the same magnitude effect on trade as the euro. Also, they find that the Rose effect is larger in the broader sample of nations. When they run their preferred estimate on EU nations only, the Rose effect drops more than two standard deviations. Moreover, the estimate for the exports of non-euro area nations to euro area nations is almost identical to the intra-euro area effect, while the euro area's exports to non-euro area nations seem to be unaffected by the new currency. This finding is both intriguing and suspicious. The intriguing part is that if it is really coming from the euro's introduction, then the euro must be making it easy, cheaper and/or safer to sell to euro area nations. Or to put it differently, the euro makes the euro area members extraordinarily good importers, rather than extraordinarily good exporters. It is suspicious since it suggests that it is not really the euro that is behind it all, but rather something that the euro area nations, or a subset of them, did around the time of the euro – something that made their markets more open to imports from all other EU nations.

Another hint that it may not have been the euro causing the big trade effect comes from the authors' experiments with the sample. The estimate of the intra-euro area dummy jumps up by about one standard deviation when the sample includes Norway and Switzerland in addition to the EU14 (Flam and Nordström seem to exclude Greece from their aggregate regressions since they lacked Greek data for the sector regressions). Moreover, the dummy on euro area exports to non-EA nations also jumps up, by two standard deviations. What could this mean?

Recall the difference-in-differences interpretation of the model estimated with pair dummies (a separate one for each direction-specific bilateral export). The treatment groups in all cases are intra-EA trade flows. What changes with the sample is the control group. In the EU sample, the control group is the six trade flows among the three 'outs', i.e. non-EA members, Britain, Denmark and Sweden, since Flam and Nordström include dummies for all trade flows between the ins and outs. Adding in Norway and Switzerland brings the total up to 20 control pairs. The fact that the EA dummy estimate rises so much reflects the fact that trade between Norway and Switzerland and between these nations and the outs did not rise as much as trade among the outs did during this period. That in itself suggests that some strongly pro-trade factor omitted from the regression was stimulating trade among EU members, regardless of the euro usage. The authors do include an EEA dummy (which stands for the European Economic Area agreement whose goal is to extend the single market to Norway and Iceland), so this should have been controlled for, but they may still be missing something. The leftmost bar in Figure 2.11 shows the year by year EA dummy; the other bar in each pair of bars shows the estimated EU dummy (actually it is the EEA dummy even though they call it the EU dummy). What we see is that just as the Rose effect is estimated to be increasing sharply, in the 1999 to 2001 period, the effectiveness of the single market is estimated as diminishing by almost as much. The line shows the sum of the two. This also 'explains' why De Souza (2002) finds no Rose effect when he includes a time trend for EU integration, and why Berger and Nitsch (2005) are able to shrink the Rose effect to nothing by including a time trend for integration among the eventual euro area members.

All this invites further study, as Berger and Nitsch would say. It might also be interesting to interact an estimated EU integration trend with individual members' transposition deficits (i.e. the extent to which they are behind in implementing EU directives). It is worrying that the outs and the ins are so different when it comes to transposition in the face of rising overall integration. It would also be interesting to see the sensitivity to period with the EU sample alone.

Exchange rates and gravity. But does it work in theory?

One of the methodological innovations in Flam and Nordström is their treatment of exchange rates. The inclusion of exchange rates is important to control one of the potential sources of spurious Rose effects in the euro data. As the euro dropped sharply at birth, the intra-euro area goods came to look cheap compared to third nation goods, US goods in particular. In other words, the exchange rate altered

Figure 2.11 Flam-Nordström estimates of Single Market and euro area dummies

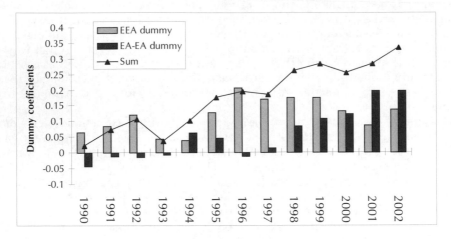

Figure 2.12 Euro against the dollar, 1999-2005

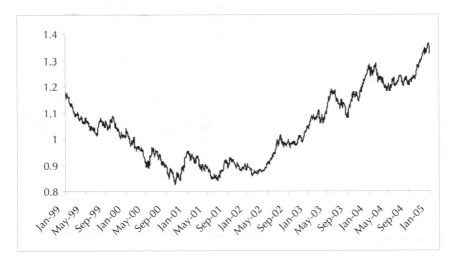

relative prices inside the euro area in a way that would boost intra-euro area trade. If one fails to control for this properly, the coefficient on the EA dummy will be biased by the omitted variable.

2.2.4 Other studies

Barr, Breedon and Miles (2003)

Barr, Breedon and Miles (2003) is another paper that was presented at the same *Economic Policy* Panel as MSO. Estimating the Rose effect was not the central axis of investigation in this paper; they try to systematically compare EU members inside and outside the euro area. Their early drafts study a wide variety of issues, but comments from referees, Managing Editors and – above all – the Panellists led them to pare down the paper to a focus on trade. For comparative purposes, they also make preliminary estimates of the effect of monetary union on three other dimensions of economic performance – foreign direct investment, the development of financial markets and overall macroeconomic performance – though they recognize that their ability to control for other factors is more limited for these other indicators.[36] These authors make a much more thorough attempt than MSO to correct for reverse causality. Even after this correction, however, they note that the Rose effect is positive and significant.

Bun and Klaassen (2002)

One of the other papers in line for the I-did-it-first prize is Bun and Klaassen (2002), since their first draft was circulated in 2001. This paper employs a dynamic fixed effects estimator. The results they obtain are quite similar to those reported for MSO using a similar estimator.

De Souza (2002), Piscitelli (2003) and De Nardis and Vicarelli (2003a)

De Souza (2002) estimates the basic gravity model for the EU15 countries with the addition of a time trend. He finds no evidence for a significant Rose effect unless he removes the trend. This result is interesting, maybe even important, but throwing linear terms can do lots of things to a regression that gets most of its traction from the time-variation of the policy variable of interest. MSO's experiments with time trends (in the first draft) and a direct measure of EU integration in the published version do not line up with De Souza's findings.

Piscitelli (2003), following the 2001 draft of MSO, finds that lengthening the sample back to 1980 reduces the Rose effect estimates. The paper also finds that the size of the Rose effect changes with the data used. OECD trade data uses the 'cost, insurance and freight' (cif) methodology while the IMF trade data used in MSO (2003) takes the 'free on board' (fob) approach. I'll have much more to say about this result, but I note here that fob is what you get when you rely on the exporter's data and cif when you rely on the importer's data (for most nations, the UN's ComTrade database – the fount of all trade data – has four observations on bilateral trade, e.g. France to Germany as reported by the French and Germans, and Germany to France again by both nations; MSO average all of these to get their one estimate of bilateral trade).

De Nardis and Vicarelli (2003a) was also one of the early papers on this. (One of the reasons *Economic Policy* decided to commission MSO was that others had found similar results.) They take a different tack at controlling for reverse causality, but get about the same answer as MSO; 10% in the short run and 20% in the long run.

Anderton, Baltagi, Skudelny and De Souza (2002)

This paper uses more sophisticated econometrics – three-stage least squares – to estimate import demand functions. They find no direct evidence of a Rose effect, but given the relatively small number of post-euro observations, it is hard to know what to make of this. Given the good data on Europe, however, this more direct approach to estimating the euro's impact should probably be tried again.

Mancini-Griffoli and Pauwels (2006)

One very recent paper uses sophisticated econometrics to identify the timing of the structural break caused by the euro. The authors develop a panel-data version of the recent end-of-sample structural break test suggested by Andrews (2003). This allows them to explicitly deal with the fact that there are very few data observations after the euro's introduction. The test avoids the need to make assumptions about the distributions of errors by building a test-statistic whose distribution is estimated using parametric subsampling techniques. One key novelty is that the power of the test allows the authors to test for short-lived breaks.

Their findings confirm those of some of some papers in the field but contradict others. First, they find that the euro did have a positive impact on trade with the effect being first felt break in the first quarter of 1999. Second, they find that the structural break is short-lived, lasting only up to mid-2001. Third, they find no evidence that the euro affected the trade of non-euro area nations – a result that contrasts with MSO (2003) and Flam and Nordström (2003) who find a positive effect for non-euro area nations.

2.3   Did the euro affect trade pricing?

The standard Mundellian optimal-currency-area story has multiple currencies acting as transaction costs – what is often called a 'frictional' trade barrier (something like a tariff where the tariff revenue is thrown away). If this traditional view is correct, then we should observe a significant impact of the euro on trade pricing. In particular, to the extent that currency-linked transaction costs are important, adoption of a common currency should narrow international price differences with the currency union, but not between the currency union and the rest of the world. More modern theories of international pricing suggest that price dispersion is limited by an 'arbitrage band' whose width may be related to exchange rate volatility and common currency (Baldwin, 1991; Baldwin and Taglioni, 2005).

So what do the data say?

While the empirical literature on the euro's trade pricing impact is severely underdeveloped compared to the trade flow literature, a string of recent studies suggest that the euro has affected trade pricing. This is a very recent development since one early and very influential study on this question – Engel and Rogers (2004) – suggested that the euro had had no impact. One major problem in this literature stems from the lack of a standard, well-estimated and widely agreed model of what trade pricing should look like. Without this trade-price-equivalent of the gravity model, the studies are difficult to interpret and compare.

We start with the papers that support the notation that the euro has had an impact on trade pricing, in particular by narrowing the price dispersion among members of the euro area.

2.3.1   Allington, Kattuman and Waldmann (2005)

Allington et al. (2005) is the best paper in the field to date, in my opinion. The authors focus on a measure of price dispersion, comparing the pre-euro and post-euro behaviour of their measure for nations that are inside the euro area and nations that are not. To control partly for many other integrating policy changes, they limit the universe to members of the EU15. They find robust results which show that the euro significantly lowered price dispersion within the euro group. The data they use is eurostat's 'Comparative price level indices' for individual consumption expenditure in about 200 product groups for all EU15 countries during 1995-2002 (annual data).

The authors also report that there was not a sudden change in dispersion, but that the euro's introduction accelerated the declining dispersion that was ongoing during the 1990s (the 1990s was marked by substance market integration in the EU). Moreover, they find enormous differences across product categories. This sort of cross-sector variation is perfectly normal in disaggregated data, but it highlights the fact that the euro's impact on economic activity is surely different in different sectors.

The key to the authors' finding is a difference-in-difference result of the sort that was discussed at length in Section 2.1. The basic idea is to see whether the change in dispersion between the pre- and post-euro periods (the 'difference') is substantially different between the euro area nations and the other EU members (the difference between the differences). The hypothesis they test is straightforward. If the euro did diminish price dispersion, the euro group's pre-versus-post difference should be bigger than the non-EA group's.

The authors' data for all their products are plotted in Figures 2.13 and 2.14. Figure 2.13 shows the products where the EA group's dispersion fell less in the post-euro period (which counts against their hypothesis). Figure 2.14 shows the products where the EA group's dispersion did fall more (as would be the case if the euro promoted price convergence).

Comparing the figures we see that while there are some products where the non-EA group saw more convergence, there were far more products where the euro seems to have promoted price convergence. The scales are the same on the two graphs so we can also compare magnitudes of the difference in differences. While most of the numbers are less than 0.05 (in absolute value) in Figure 2.13, about half the numbers are greater than those in the products where the EA group saw greater convergence. What all this suggests is that the euro does seem to have promoted price convergence in the euro group, although the effect is clearly not overwhelming.

2.3.2 Supporting papers

Beck and Weber (2003) look at prices in 81 cities and 10 types of goods during 1991-2002. They find that monetary union significantly reduced cross-border relative price volatility. The effect, however, is not immediate and certainly not complete (national borders and distance still matter). Evidence from the German unification experience and the early phase of EMU suggests that relative price convergence is relatively fast. They find that the half-life of the East-West German price level convergence was between 1.5 and 2 years. Their findings for the first years of the euro suggest that price level convergence had already occurred to a large extent by 2002 (roughly 80% of the initial relative price dispersion had been eliminated by 2002). Readers may be interested to know that Weber from Beck and Weber (2003) is now President of the Bundesbank.

Isgut (2002) finds similar results using two balanced panels of 116 cities and 69 goods and 79 cities and 123 goods in 2001, and concluded that the same currency reduces price differences generally by 2-3% (using standard deviations of log price differences across city pairs) and in the EMU specifically, by 5%, even when EU had been controlled for.

The impact of currency union is confirmed by Lutz (2003) using data on the Belgium-Luxembourg currency union (set up in 1953) and the rest of the EU. He focuses on price convergence for 90 automobile models during 1993-98. His econometrics suggest 4% lower price differential within the currency union even when the other determinants of economic integration had been controlled.

Yet another study confirming the Allington et al. (2005) results is Foad (2005). This paper uses an original dataset, namely monthly data on prices facing US State Department employees living abroad as reflected in their permitted per diem for lodging, meals and incidental expenses for 201 cities in 16 countries, from 1995 to 2002. The author finds that the impact of the euro on cross-border price volatility varied by country size. Within the euro area, cross-border price volatility did not change between the small countries, but fell significantly between the large euro area countries.

Imbs et al. (2004) use a unique dataset on television prices across European countries and regions. They find that euro area members display lower price dispersion than non-EMU countries and that regional price dispersion is comparable to intra-EMU dispersion.

Figure 2.13 Panel A: Difference in differences, EA and non-EA EU **members**

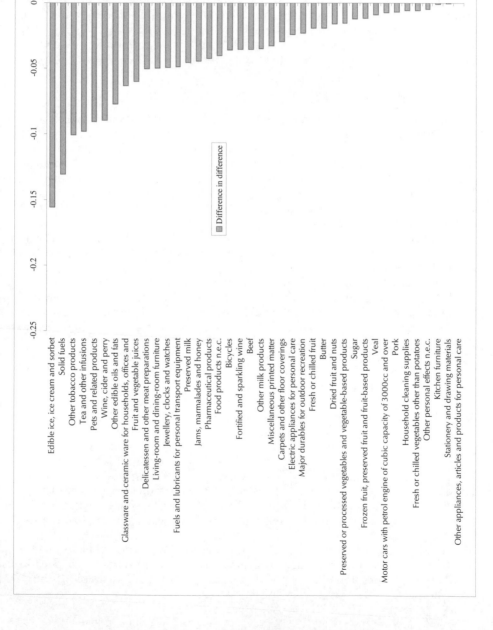

Figure 2.14 Panel B: Difference in differences, EA and non-EA EU members

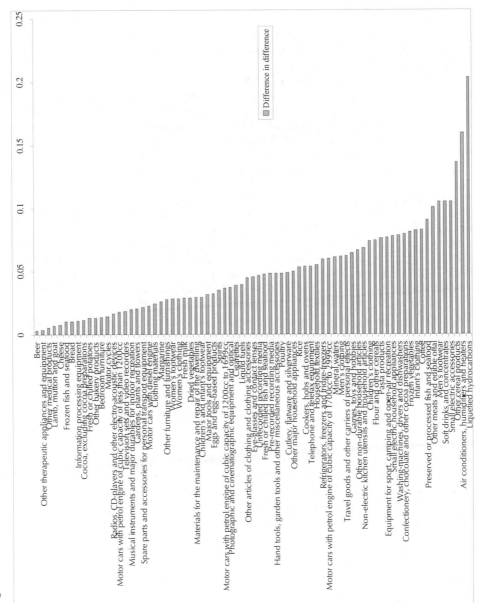

2.3.3 The odd man out: Engel and Rogers (2004)

When the *Economic Policy* Managing Editors decided in April 2002 to do a whole Panel on the euro's effects, one natural topic was the euro's impact on trade prices. We eventually got Charles Engel, Michel Knetter and John Rogers to agree to do a paper on the topic, but the paper experienced a number of difficulties before it was eventually published in July 2004. Knetter had to withdraw as he became a Dean and neither Engel nor Rogers could make the euro-issue Panel, so the paper was not published with the others in the *Economic Policy* special issue on the euro that also appeared as the book by Baldwin, Bertola and Seabright (2003). The paper that was eventually published as Engel and Rogers (2004) was presented at the October 2003 *Economic Policy* Panel in Rome. The Rome Panel was highly critical of the paper – the main critiques were published in the Discussants' and Panellists' comments along with the paper – so the Managing Editors asked for major revisions that delayed the paper longer than *Economic Policy*'s usual 6-months-after-the-panel rule. Even with the delay, it was one of the first papers to look at the price effects using a significant number of post-euro observations.

Specifically, Engel and Rogers (2004) use data gathered by the Economists Intelligence Unit on consumers prices of 101 traded goods and 38 non-traded items in 18 European cities (11 in euro area countries and 7 in non-euro area countries) for the years 1990-2003. This price data, which was collected to help firms decide upon the cost-of-living adjustment they should offer to expatriate employees, concerns individual goods and care is taken to ensure that the goods are comparable and the prices are for similar outlets (e.g. high-street stores in all the cities rather than large discount chains in one city and a boutique store in another).

The authors find no evidence that the euro decreased price dispersion among euro area members, although they do find that there has been a significant reduction in price dispersion throughout the decade of the 1990s.

Why do Engel and Rogers (2004) find such different results? A look at their data and the critique of one of their discussants at the Panel, Giovanni Veronese from the Bank of Italy, is revealing. The authors take as their measure of price dispersion the mean squared error of the log difference in prices between cities. The salient points from the cross-section aspect of the raw data are:

- Price dispersion is greater among non-euro nations than it is among the Euro-11.

- Price dispersion among both euro and non-euro nations is greater than members of the DM bloc (a group that experienced very little exchange rate variability in the 10 years leading up to the Euro's introduction).

- Price dispersion across cities within a single nation is even lower than that of the DM bloc.

On the face of it, these cross-group comparisons suggest that the level of price dispersion is roughly correlated with the degree of exchange rate variability.

The time series facts, however, seem to tell a different story. Price dispersion in all four groups shows a clear decline in the early 1990s, but the decline stops around the time of the euro's introduction. Indeed, it even seems to increase somewhat. Thus the time-series facts seem to suggest that the euro had no impact on price dispersion, or even raised the degree of dispersion.

The problem with this conclusion, and the main point of Giovanni Veronese, was that these results are not conditional on other factors. In particular, Veronese suggests that there was a powerful force driving increased dispersion in the post-1999 period, namely the divergence of national inflation rates in the euro area that occurred just after the euro's launch.

Figure 2.15 Engel and Rogers (2004), price dispersion data by group

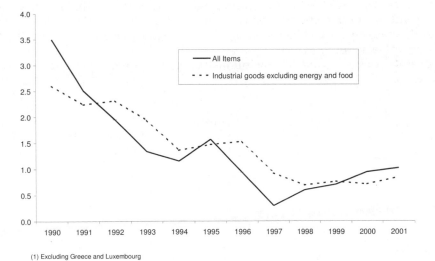

Source: Engel and Rogers (2004), Figure 4

Figure 2.16 Convergence and divergence of euro area inflation rates, 1990-2001

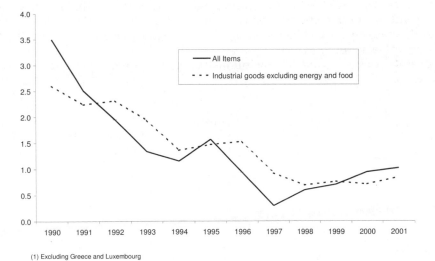

(1) Excluding Greece and Luxembourg

Veronese's evidence is shown in Figure 2.16. The big-push to meet the Maastricht criteria led to a substantial drop in euro area nations' inflation. In the figure this shows up as a drop in the standard deviation of inflation rates since they were all converging on the three lowest rates as per the criteria. However, once the list of 'winners' was announced a number of euro nations relaxed their efforts and inflation rates diverged again.

The diverging inflation rates should have been reflected in an increased dispersion of prices. Moreover, since this belt-tightening-and-loosening exercise was not undertaken by the non-euro nations, one should have expected to see a greater rise in the euro area's price dispersion than that of the non-euro area. From Figure 2.15 however, we see the euro area's dispersion rose no more and perhaps less than that of the non-Euro nations.

Of course controlling for this sort of factor is exactly what the econometrics is for, but Engel and Rogers (2004) do not consider domestic inflation to be a factor. As Veronese says in his published comment on the paper:

> Regarding the empirical analysis, my comments concerned mainly the lack of a clear motivation as to why they conduct a fully fledged regression analysis, after having found unconditionally that no price level convergence occurred after 1998. The authors seem to argue that controlling for 'other' factors in their regressions EMU might have played a positive role in the convergence of prices. However the factors they control for (income per capita, taxes, etc) are not a priori expected to play a counteractive role, and therefore to mask the effective role of EMU.

> In particular their claim, 'Even controlling for these other factors, Euro does not seem to matter', seems out of place since, a priori I would have expected to find nothing new with respect to the unconditional results. The potential sources of divergence, such as differences in national inflation rates, are not included in their regressions.

Some of other earlier studies, such as, Parsley and Wei (2001), also find no euro effect, but this is not in contradiction to the later positive findings since their data stops at 2000, and papers such as Allington et al. (2005) suggest that the euro's price effect does not involve a jump in 1999.

For completeness, I include a table summarizing all the most relevant studies (see Appendix A).

3   Is the Euro Area Rose Effect a Spurious Result?

While the size of the estimated euro area Rose effect does not strain credibility in the same way as the bigger estimates in the earlier literature did, many questions remain. The speed with which the effect appears is suspicious, as is the fact that it appeared before 1999 according to several researchers. The lack of a trade diversion effect also raises questions.

It is always exciting to find something new and real, but one must also consider the possibility that the effect is spurious. I believe there to be three hypotheses that need to be eliminated before we can be absolutely sure that the estimates are telling us anything real about the economy.

- VAT fraud created a spurious Rose effect.

- Delayed effects of the euro depreciation created a spurious Rose effect.

- Effects of euro area implementation of Internal Market measures create a spurious Rose effect.

These are considered in turn.

3.1   Lies, damned lies and statistics: VAT fraud

This section considers the very real possibility that the Rose effect in the euro area is a statistical illusion stemming from the way trade figures are gathered. This is headache material, but I believe it is necessary since existing estimates of the effects are of the same order of magnitude as the estimated Rose effects in the euro area.

One of the great coups of the 1986 Single European Act was to remove Europe's internal borders, at least as far as trade is concerned. This happened in 1993 and changed the way trade statistics were gathered on intra-EU trade. Data on intra-EU trade from 1993 onwards were collected by VAT authorities rather than customs officers, since intra-EU trade no longer passed through customs frontiers.

Why would VAT authorities produce trade statistics? EU nations have VAT systems that are based on the so-called destination principle, i.e. a good pays the VAT rate of the nation where it is sold, not where it is made. Practically speaking, this means that the exporting EU nation rebates its VAT to the exporting firm and the importing EU member imposes its own VAT rate on the importing firm. This is why VAT authorities have always kept track of imports and exports.

The problem is that this creates a direct link between trade date and tax avoidance and evasion. Worse still, tax enforcement changes – and anticipation of the same – can create reactions that distort EU trade flows. These distortions can vary across time, across trade pairs and commodities. Although the VAT system was massively reformed in anticipation of the suppression of border controls – a major part of this being a narrowing of differences in VAT rates – the 1993 system was susceptible to fraud.

Box 3.1: Acquisition and carousel fraud

The easiest fraud is called acquisition fraud. Criminals set up a company in, say, the UK and import goods from Germany at a zero-VAT price (the selling company gets the Germany VAT rebated). The importing firm sells the goods in Britain at something like the with-VAT price (since that is what honest importers have to charge) but they never pay the VAT; they go out of business before the VAT authorities can get them.

The carousel fraud takes this one step further, but understanding it requires some background on why VAT is usually impervious to fraud. An EU firm that sells a good is liable for the VAT on the full sales price, unless entrepreneurs can prove that they bought inputs to make the good, in which case they only pay the VAT on their value added. The point is that the VAT has already been paid on the inputs. How do we know the VAT has been paid on inputs? Well, whether it was made locally or imported, the local VAT rate was paid. How do we know that the firm won't exaggerate its purchases of inputs? Counteracting incentives is the answer. The input seller would like to under-report its sales to reduce its VAT bill, but the input buyer would like to over-report its purchases to reduce its VAT bill. The gain and loss are of identical magnitude, so there is no reason to suspect an upward or downward bias. In short, buyers and sellers become informants on each other as far as VAT payments are concerned. Now, how does this work with exports? Suppose the export shipment is to Belgium and is worth £100,000. If the UK VAT rate is 20%, the British VAT authority pays the exporting firm £20,000 - which is the amount of VAT that has been paid on the good in Britain.

But what if the VAT was never paid on the import into Britain because of an acquisition fraud? In this case, the criminals pocket £20,000, having paid very little, or maybe no VAT, in Britain. Since it worked once, they may be tempted to put the same goods through the same cycle again. The goods turn around and around like a carousel, each time showing up twice as an export and once or never as an import.

3.1.1 Fraud and intra-EU trade figures

As early as the mid-1990s, problems of VAT fraud were recognized, for example, by the European Parliament's first Temporary Enquiry Committee in 1997. Measures were taken to improve the system, but things were still problematic when the euro was launched. A European Commission report to the Council and European Parliament in 2000 used usually blunt language:

> The transitional VAT arrangements have been in place for more than 6 years. During this period, one would have expected that the implementing problems should have been solved and that the system should be running smoothly. However, this does not appear to be the case. The 6 years appear to have given the fraudsters time to appreciate the possibilities offered by the transitional VAT arrangements to make money, while, generally speaking, Member States have not met the challenge posed by fraud. ...There are indications that the level of serious fraud in intra-Community trade is growing.

The exact nature of such fraud is not easy to ascertain. Typically, it creates a gap between export statistics (every exporter wants the VAT rebate) and import statistics (some have an incentive to avoid paying the importing nation's VAT). But, it can also inflate the trade statistics as in the case of the so-called 'carousel fraud' (see Box 3.1).

3.1.2 The effect is huge and anti-fraud activity differs across time and country pairs

The effect of this fraud was so large that the UK had to restate its national accounts (see Ruffles et al., 2003). The revisions involve upward adjustments to imports of £1.7 billion in 1999, £2.8 billion in 2000, £7.1 billion in 2001 and £11.1 billion in 2002. Unadjusted imports in 2002 were £220 billion, so the effect is about 5%. The problem is not limited to the UK as Figure 3.1 shows. The problem is large, on the order of 5%, and it varies over time. As inspection of the figure shows, the problem appears to increase substantially in the run up to the Euro's introduction.

Policy reaction is correlated with the timing of the Euro's introduction. The European Commission has been coordinating the implementation of anti-fraud activities since the 1990s, and these are still not complete. The rate of implementation varies across nations and across types of trade. I presume the criminals involved in this fraud follow the process carefully, so it is entirely possible that they alter their behaviour in anticipation of changes.

If this fraud were simple – e.g. it consisted entirely of acquisition fraud, simple fixes might work, for example, researchers could use export data. But as the carousel fraud suggests, even these data may be exaggerated in ways that vary across time, country pairs and commodities.

Figure 3.1 Difference between intra-EU exports and imports

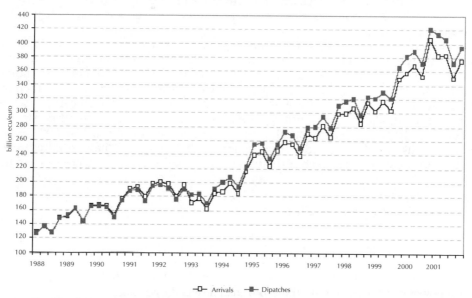

3.2 The Rotterdam effect

A huge fraction of Germany's imports from non-EU nations arrive via Rotterdam. Some of this trade is recorded as a Dutch import from, say, New Zealand and then recorded as a German import from the Netherlands. Some of it, however, is recorded as a German import from New Zealand since it is subject to a 'transit' regime by which the tariff and VAT are not paid until the good arrives in Germany. The system is called the TIR system ('Transports Internationaux Routiers') and it involves transferring sealed containers from ships to trucks (Rotterdam and Antwerp are the big centres for this, but it happens at other ports as well).

The removal of fiscal border checks within the EU teamed with the rapid rise in the volume of trade, made fraud a big problem in the EU. Anti-fraud measures lead to a reaction that resulted in a rise in the amount of third nation goods being declared twice, once as an import into Holland and once as an export from Holland to the true destination. There are a million stories, but here is one that gives an inkling of the problem: as a European Commission pamphlet on the EU's transit system tells it:

> In the early 1990s, the TIR system also began to experience a significant increase in fraud leading to large losses of duties and charges. Much of the fraud concerned tobacco and alcohol, both subject to high rates of duties and charges. In those cases the US$50,000 limit of the guarantee was often inadequate to meet claims made by customs. A special 'tobacco/alcohol' guarantee of US$200,000 was therefore introduced on 1 January 1994. The situation was so bad that, with effect from 30 November 1994, the central pool of insurers were forced to withdraw their insurance cover for all guarantees for tobacco and alcohol. This meant it was no longer possible to move tobacco and alcohol under TIR. Furthermore, with effect from 1 April 1996, the national associations of some Community Member States withdrew their TIR guarantees for those sensitive goods that were banned from using the comprehensive guarantee in Community transit, for example beef, milk, cream and butter. As a result it is impossible for these goods to move under TIR into or out of the Community.

Of course, if these goods don't use the TIR, the intra-EU trade rises relative to the extra-EU trade. The point is that before and after the good is counted as being imported once from the third nation, but afterwards it is also counted as trade between Holland and Germany. Observant readers will remember that Flam and Nordström (2003) found that the Rose effect was largest in tobacco and alcohol.

As with the VAT fraud, one could image simple fixes if the problem were simple, but unfortunately the magnitude of the problem varies over time and by member state. The worst part is that EU attempts to address this fraud have been phased in tandem with the Euro. The transit regime reform has three phases, the first starting in February 1999, the second starting in spring 2002 and the third in 2003. Since these reforms are likely to reduce transit fraud, they may well have resulted in an increase in reported trade, even if there was no increase, or even a decrease in trade.

3.3 PECS: woes with ROOs

The next problem with the statistics comes from another highly technical consideration – Rules of Origin, or ROOs.

The EU is the world champion when it comes to preferential trade agreements. These cover not only intra-EU trade but also a very large share of EU imports from third nations ranging from Switzerland to Mexico. Preferential trade agreements, however, only cut tariffs on goods originating in nations that have signed the agreement. To establish which goods get the tariff preference these agreements need 'rules of origin'.

Throughout my career as a trade economist, I've tried to ignore ROOs for two good reasons: they are dauntingly complex and mind-numbingly dull. My third reason for ignoring them – they don't matter much – turns out to be wrong. A string of recent papers demonstrates that they do affect trade flows, i.e. they are non-tariff barriers. In a recent paper in Economic Policy, Augier et al. (2005), study the impact of ROOs on European trade. In particular, they study the impact of a change in which the EU applies its ROOs. This change, known as the Pan-European Cumulation System (PECS), was implemented in 1997.

The system is complex, but it was set up at the request of EU industry to reduce the existing complexity. Here's how. Staying competitive requires firms to set up a complex supply chain in which components were shipped among many nations. In the mid-1990s, there were something like 60 bilateral FTAs in Europe, each with its own complex set of origin rules. Such complexity made it difficult for firms to optimize manufacturing structures: it was hard if not impossible for a firm to be absolutely sure on how the outsourcing of one of its intermediate goods would affect the origin status of its final-good exports.

The PECS simplified this in two ways: (1) it imposed uniform rules of origin in the EU15, EFTA nations and the ten nations that joined the EU in 2004; and (2) it allowed firms to count goods from any of these nations as originating in the EU.

Theoretically, the biggest impact on trade flows is between 'spoke' economies that had FTAs with the EU, but it could also encourage or discourage EU imports from non-EU nations – both those that are part of PECS and those who aren't (see Augier et al., 2005).

The relevance here is that this could alter trade flows in the EU just about the time the euro was introduced. Augier et al. (2005), for example, found that PECS had a statistically significant impact on trade flows between the EU and non-EU PECS nations (both ways), and as well as boosting trade among the spokes. It is also not exactly clear whether PECS could warp the way in which EU imports are allocated across third nations.

3.4 Euro depreciation and appreciation

Another suspect for spurious results is the sharp depreciation of the euro at its birth. Here is the basic story. The gravity equation is a fancy demand curve. The sudden and sharp depreciation of the euro between 1999 and 2001 would make intra-euro area goods look cheaper relative to the extra-euro area goods. If this is not properly controlled for, the EA dummy would pick up the expenditure-shifting effect and report it as a Rose effect. Flam and Nordström attempt to control for this, but they have not addressed the problem of lags. Given the usual lags involved in trade, the impact on trade flows could last for a couple of years and thus still bias the results. Another point concerns the differential external exposures of euro area nations to external trade. For example, Greece does much less trade with the dollar zone than Ireland, so the euro depreciation could be behind part of the differential effects that MSO find.

3.5 Delayed Single Market effects

As the papers by Berger and Nitsch (2005) and Mongelli et al. (2005) show, European integration is a work in progress. The doorstep to the Euro, the 1992 to 1998 period, witnessed a particularly intense burst of deeper integration for all members. This would not have been a problem for the Flam and Nordström or MSO estimates done on the EU sample, if only all EU members had introduced these Single Market measures at the same time. But 'if only' is the bane of empirical economics. EU members differ widely on their pace of implementing EU Directives. More to the point, most of the 'tortoises' are inside the euro area and most of the 'hares' are outside, and the tortoises made a substantial catch-up effort in the run up to monetary union, as Figure 3.2 shows. (See Box 3.2 for a discussion of what the IMI shows exactly.)

If you combine this with the likelihood that the pro-trade effects of many Directives may take a couple of years or more to be fully realized, it is easy to see that there is a real problem. It is possible that the 'euro effect' is nothing more than the delayed and differential effect of pro-trade directives.

Figure 3.2 Internal Market Index evolution euro area (EA) versus non-euro area (non-EA)

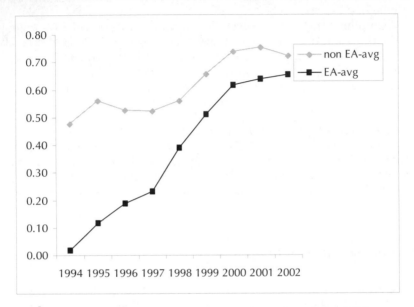

Source: 'The Internal Market Index 2004', DG Joint Research, European Commission (2004).

Box 3.2: The Internal Market Index (IMI)

The index used in Figure 3.2 is calculated by the European Commission in order to track the effects of Internal Market policy. The Index does not focus on measures of medium-term results which can be more directly linked to policy action. It is computed as a weighted sum of 12 base indicators - their relative importance was decided by canvassing the members of the Internal Market Advisory Committee (IMAC), the group of Member State officials who advise the Commission on Internal Market matters. The base indicators and their weight are shown below.

IMI sub-component	Weight (%)	IMI sub-component	Weight (%)
Sectoral and ad hoc state aid	14	Retail lending interest rates over savings rate	4
Value of pension fund assets	1	Intra-EU foreign direct investment (FDI)	12
Telecommunication costs	9	Intra-EU trade	14
Electricity prices	12	Workers from other Member States	3
Gas prices	7	Value of published public procurement	13
Relative price level	10	Postal tariffs	1

Note: This box is based on European Commission (2004).

3.6   Bottom line

Here I end my 'Doubting Thomas' digression. All three of the sources for spurious results should be taken seriously by empirical researchers, but I believe a Rose effect happened. Apart from the econometric evidence reviewed above, my belief is bolstered by anecdotal evidence in abundance. Just tell any group of European businesspeople – especially ones who own small or medium enterprises – that the euro had no impact on trade inside Europe. After a guffaw, you will almost surely hear 'of course, it did'. Now it is time to think about the microeconomics of why.

4 What Caused the Euro Area Rose Effect?

This is indeed a mystery. What do you imagine that it means?' Watson remarked. 'I have no data yet. It is a capital mistake to theorize before one has data. Insensibly one begins to twist facts to suit theories, instead of theories to suit facts. (Sherlock Holmes, *A Scandal in Bohemia*)

I believe that we can be fairly sure that some form of Rose effect is occurring in the euro area. The cleanest test in my opinion is the Flam and Nordström (2003) estimate using only EU members on data from 1989 to 2002. Since they put in pair dummies using direction-specific exports, they have controlled for all time-invariant idiosyncratic relationships among the EU15, and reduced the risk of biases from the underreporting of imports. Because the time period is relatively short, the serial correlation, that we know must be in their residuals, should not pose too much of a problem in terms of biasing the point estimate of the Rose effect. And most importantly, because they only use EU members that have not joined the euro area, they have controlled for most of the bias that might emerge from unobserved pro- or anti-trade policies adopted by the EU in tandem with the euro's introduction. It would be useful to see a few more sensitive tests, but this result, combined with similar findings by MSO, Berger-Nitsch and many others, leads me to believe that the Rose effect is for real in the euro area.

If I had to provide 'the' number, I would – after plenty of provisos about the Rose effect not being a magic wand – say the number is 9% for intra-euro area trade and 7% for exports to the euro area by outsiders based on the Flam-Nordström findings. It would, however, be hard to argue against any number between 5% and 15% for either of these figures. We do not really know enough to say whether the long-term effect will be substantially higher.

This chapter does three things. It collects the various clues from the empirical literature, it provides a framework for thinking about the possible causes of the euro area Rose effect, and finally it uses the framework and the clues to argue that the extra trade is most likely to be in new goods, probably from small and medium size firms, rather than increased sales of existing products.

4.1 Collection of clues

This section attempts to draw critical clues from the empirical literature, that is to say, to stylize the facts in a way that helps us think about the causes of the Rose effect. I organize the clues into spatial clues, timing clues and sector clues.

4.1.1   Spatial variation of the euro area Rose effect

The MSO (2003b) and Flam and Nordström (2003) papers report extensive robustness checks, and many of these contain critical clues as to what might be causing the Rose effect. Deep within the MSO paper are nation-by-nation estimates of the Rose effect for each euro area nation. Figure 4.1 converts MSO's raw coefficients into percent increases in trade and plots the results by nation. The nations are ordered by decreasing Rose effect. Three features are particularly relevant.[37]

(1) Apart from Spain, the nations with the highest Rose effects are those that are already the most tightly integrated: the Benelux nations and Germany.

These nations have been in an informal, but very tight exchange rate arrangement called the DM-bloc for decades. Intra-DM bloc volatility was very low, so the euro had only a very small impact on the bilateral exchange rate variability among these nations. This is a bit puzzling since one might have thought that the trade effects would have been largest among nations that had the largest, pre-euro bilateral volatility.

(2) These nations are geographically proximate, so we suppose that the natural trade costs among these nations are quite low; gravity model estimates in Europe suggest that each doubling of the distance between capitals lowers trade by about 70%. Moreover, these nations are among the most avid integrationists in the EU and thus have embraced the EU's deep trade integration even more tightly than other members.

For example, the Benelux nations formed a customs union even before the EU was founded in 1958, and Belgium and Luxembourg have shared a common currency since just after the war. As part of this distance-Rose-effect nexus, we note that the size of the euro's trade impact is lowest in the geographically peripheral euro area

Figure 4.1 The euro's trade effect by nation

Source: Baldwin and Taglioni (2004), based on Micco et al. (2003), Table 8.

nations: Greece, Portugal, Finland and Ireland. Again this suggests a negative relationship between trade costs and the Rose effect.

(3) Berger and Nitsch (2005) point out that estimates of the Rose effect on an EU sample that excludes the DM bloc turn out to be insignificant. In other words, the effect is not just strong in these countries, the aggregate numbers like 5% to 10% are actually driven entirely by these nations.

The fact can be read in two ways. Pessimistically, it says that it is not the euro, but some unobserved policy adopted by DM bloc nations that is driving the results. But what could it be: general product and labour market reforms that Britain, Denmark and Sweden had already undertaken? Optimistically, it could be that exactly because these nations had such low exchange rate volatility for so long, their firms were in a good position to profit from the removal of small costs. If this is right, we should see the Rose effect appearing in the non-DM euro area members, but more slowly.

4.1.2 Trade with non-euro area nations: lack of trade diversion

Intriguingly, MSO (2003b) find that trade between euro area nations and other nations rose with the euro's introduction, but not quite as much. Specifically, they estimate what might be called a one-sided euro dummy (EMU 1) which value is unity for any trading pair that involves only one euro area member (the regular euro dummy, or two-sided dummy EMU 2, is only for trading pairs where both nations are in the euro area). The results in their two datasets (one for EU nations only and one that also includes some European and non-European nations who are not in the EU) are shown in Table 4.1.

Table 4.1 Trade diversion results, MSO (2003)

1992-2002	Dev. sample	EU
EMU 2	0.126	0.084
	(0.019)***	(0.030)***
EMU 1	0.086	0.012
	(0.015)***	(0.030)
Real GDP	-0.008	0.048
	(0.021)	(0.030)
Free trade agreement	0.030	-0.044
	(0.022)	(0.053)
EU	0.000	-0.001
	(0.001)	(0.004)
EU trend	1.108	1.071
	(0.059)***	(0.077)***
Real exchange rate of country 1	-0.220	-0.134
	(0.045)***	(0.061)**
Real exchange rate of country 2	-0.288	0.367
	(0.057)***	(0.099)***
EMU 2 impact	0.134	0.088
Transformed S.E. (delta method)	(0.015)***	(0.029)***
EMU 1 impact	0.090	0.012
Transformed S.E. (delta method)	(0.016)***	(0.029)
Observations	2541	1001
Within R2	0.46	0.65
Pair country dummies	Yes	Yes
Year dummies	Yes	Yes

Notes: Robust standard errors in parentheses. *Significant at 10%; **significant at 5%; ***significant at 1%.

On the developed country sample the estimated pro-trade effect of the euro is estimated to be about 13%, while it is only 9% on the EU sample. Since MSO cannot fully control the ongoing implementation of Single Market policies (they try with the EU Trend which is just a simple time trend for all EU trade pairs), some of the pro-trade effects of Single-Market liberalization are in the residual. The positive correlation between this residual and the included EMU 2 and EMU 1 dummies bias upward their estimates of the euro's trade effect.

One way to control for this bias is to use only trading pairs when we know the Single Market policies are in effect; we cannot identify the impact of the policy, but the time dummies sop up much of the pro-trade effect so less is left in the residual to bias the coefficients of interest. In short, the trade impact is much smaller when we control for ongoing EU liberalization. Note that given the limited variation and small number of post-euro data points, the standard errors are much larger in the EU sample. In fact the EMU 1 dummy is not significantly different to zero.

MSO also estimate the one-sided and two-sided dummies for each EA nation. The results, translated into percent increase in trade, are shown as the light bars in Figure 4.1. Roughly speaking, the one-sided impact is lower than the two-sided effect, but the nations with large two-sided effects also seem to have large one-sided effects.

This result is intriguing. It provides a very significant hint as to the microeconomics of the Rose effect, or at least as to what it is not. Informal discussion of the trade effects of a monetary union typically refer to 'transaction costs' of having different currencies. In standard trade policy terminology, having a common currency is like reducing bilateral, non-tariff barriers. The evidence on the one-sided dummy tends to reject this view. If one could model the trade-reducing effects of volatility as a frictional trade barrier, the one-sided dummy should have been negative. The euro would have been akin to a discriminatory liberalization and this should have reduced the exports of non-euro nations to the euro area.

Flam and Nordström (2003) refine this clue by estimating direction-specific trade flows. In their cleanest regression – the one that only includes EU members – they find that EA members have higher than expected imports from non-EA members, but not higher exports. Indeed, the rise in exports from non-EA members is statistically identical to the rise in exports between EA members. If one averaged the EA imports with non-EA members and EA-exports to non-members, as MSO do, then it would seem that having one half of a trade pair inside the euro area increased trade by one half the amount that it would if both partners were inside the euro area.

To see this, I reproduce some of their key regression results. The first column in Table 4.2 shows the estimate of their three euro area (EA) dummies on a sample of 20 rich nations, 13 of which are in the EU (Belgium's and Luxembourg's data are fused and Greece is dropped for data availability reasons). The dummy EA11 indicates a trade pair where both use the euro, EA10 is where the origin-nation uses the euro but not the destination-nation (this picks up outward external trade creation), and EA01 is the opposite where the destination-nation is a euro-user but the origin nation is not (this picks up inward external trade creation). The second column excludes all non-European nations from the sample and the third column excludes all non-EU nations.

As with MSO (2003), Flam and Nordström are plagued by the confluence of Single Market policy implementation and the euro's adoption. Since they cannot control for the latter, the Rose effect estimates in the first two columns are contaminated by cross effects, and since Single Market policy implementation and euro adoption or both pro-trade and positively correlated with each other, the point estimates are upward biased. This means that only the final column gives us a clean estimate of the euro's impact as opposed to the combined impact of (unmeasured) Single Market implementation and the euro's adoption.

In the final column – the best estimates – the intra-EA Rose effect is much smaller, only about 9% (0.088) and the external trade creation is only inward and is equal to about 7% (0.071). The coefficient for EA exporters to the 'outs' is close to zero (0.8%) and not statistically significant. These are what I consider to be the best estimates of the pro-trade effects of the euro. Of course readers can see that the other estimates suggest that the euro boosted the EA's external exports as much as it boosted its external imports, but I believe these estimates are biased. Specifically, I believe they assign to the euro dummy an influence that should properly be assigned to (unmeasured) Single Market policies that give EA's exports an edge in non-EU markets.

Table 4.2 Internal and external trade creation, Flam and Nordström (2003) estimates

	All nations	Only European nations	Only EU nations
EA11	0.139***	0.114***	0.088***
	(0.020)	(0.025)	(0.025)
EA10	0.077***	0.064***	0.008
	(0.017)	(0.023)	(0.027)
EA01	0.072***	0.071***	0.071***
	(0.018)	(0.024)	(0.025)
ln(RYi)	1.222***	1.214***	1.194***
	(0.071)	(0.083)	(0.080)
ln(RYj)	1.146***	1.077***	0.990***
	(0.069)	(0.074)	(0.072)
ln(REXRij)	-1.058***	-1.119***	-1.292***
	(0.050)	(0.066)	(0.063)
ln(REXRcj)	0.722***	1.026***	1.024***
	(0.067)	(0.080)	(0.083)
nomexr	-0.940**	-1.257***	-1.460***
	(0.443)	(0.448)	(0.448)
eunew	0.013	0.001	-0.002
	(0.013)	(0.013)	(0.012)
UR	0.105***		
	(0.018)		
obs	4732	2912	2184
panels	338	208	156
R2	0.99	0.99	0.99

Notes: Robust standard errors in parentheses. *Significant at 10%; **significant at 5%; ***significant at 1%. Year, EU membership, 'Rotterdam effect' and bilateral (fixed effects) dummies included but not reported. RY is real GDP, REXR are real exchange rates (bilateral and effective), nomexr is a measure of bilateral exchange rate volatility and eunew picks up the EU membership of Sweden, Finland and Austria; UR is the Uruguay Round dummy.

This is a powerful clue, if it is true. It suggests that the euro has acted more like a unilateral trade liberalization than a preferential trade liberalization. If it is true, it also has some very important implications for the politics of euro area enlargement. I'll have a lot more to say about these in Chapter 5 because it reverses some of the underpinnings of OCA theory. In basic OCA theory, you have to give up your monetary autonomy to get the benefits of reduced transaction costs. If this result is right, it suggests that Britain, Denmark and Sweden were the clever ones from a mercantilist perspective – they got the better market access without sacrificing their main macro-policy tool.

4.1.3 Timing of the euro area Rose effect

Monetary union in Europe was never a sure thing until it actually happened. Although the Treaty that laid out the path to the euro was signed in 1992, the Maastricht Treaty had several major difficulties in becoming law. Moreover, the Treaty laid down a series of conditions – the famous Maastricht conditions – for membership in the monetary union, and most European nations had trouble meeting these. Right up to the announcement of the names of the inaugural members in March 1998, sceptics doubted that the monetary union would ever become a reality.

The effect appears in 1998

Given this, the speed with which the euro's trade impact appeared is striking. Evidence for this comes from the MSO and Flam-Nordström estimates. The results are illustrated in Figure 4.2, which shows the estimated year-by-year dummies for intra-euro area trade; the dark bars show the estimates for the sample that includes only EU nations and the light bars show the estimates for the sample that includes all industrialized nations. The main points are that the Rose effect jumps up and becomes statistically significant in 1998, the year before the monetary union was formed. It jumps up again in 2001, especially for the EU sample, the year before the monetary union became a currency union.

Figure 4.2 The euro's trade effect over time

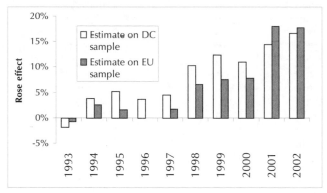

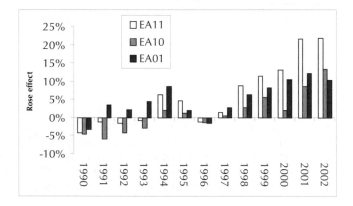

Source: Top panel: Micco et al. (2003); bottom panel: Flam and Nordström (2004).
Notes: Top panel shows the intra-EA Rose effect estimated on a broad sample of developed nations (light bars) and EU nations (dark bars). Bottom panel: the first bar is the intra-euro area, the second is euro area exports to others, the third is euro area imports from others.

Figure 4.3 Indices of European integration over time

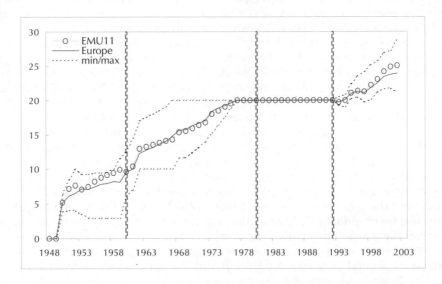

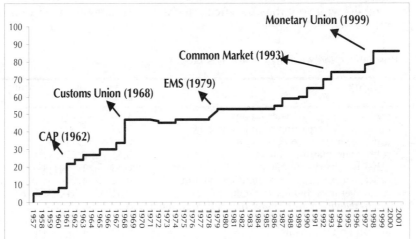

Source: Top panel: Berger and Nitsch (2005); bottom panel: Mongelli et al. (2005).

The rapid reaction of trade flows is quite remarkable since the MSO and Flam-Nordström papers control for the main determinants of bilateral trade. The speed also provides us with an important hint as to what is not going on here. Such a rapid increase in trade would be very hard to explain if, for example, it was driven by the construction of new plants related to the unwinding of hedging-related foreign direct investment.

Sensitivity to the period of estimation

Another clue relates to the nexus between the size of the estimated Rose effect and the sample period. The original draft MSO sent to Economic Policy six months before they presented the paper in Athens used two data samples, one from 1980 to 2002 and one from 1992 to 2002. Although the regressions have some serious problems that may vitiate the results, the early MSO seems to find that the Rose effect is bigger when a longer dataset is used. Berger and Nitsch (2005) confirm this result when they extend the period back to 1948 and push it forward one more year to include 2003. The finding that the Rose effect was bigger for samples starting further back is highly suspicious. It suggests that the various dummies for EU integration are not really removing everything but the euro from the data. Figure 4.3 shows that European economic integration has been an ongoing process for the last 50 years. The top panel is from Berger and Nitsch (2005) and the bottom panel is from Mongelli et al. (2005). Both show that economic integration was rising steeply just before the introduction of the euro. If pro-trade adjustments to pre-euro area integration take time, it could very well be that the lagged effects of Single Market measures are showing up in the post-1999 data and being confused with the trade effects of the euro.

At the heart of this suspicion is a mis-specification of the lags and the role of European integration. In principle this is testable and correctable with proper econometrics. For example, Flam and Nordström (2003) allow for a time-varying EU dummy and they find that their Rose effect estimate is affected very little by a change in their sample period. In any case, the diagram showing the Flam-Nordström results for the EA dummy and EU dummy suggests that it may be quite difficult to tease apart the effects of general European integration and the euro per se. Indeed, Berger and Nitsch (2005) go so far as to argue that since a time trend for integration among the euro area members wipes out the Rose effect, the MSO estimates are due to a mis-specification.

Table 4.3 Rose effect and volatility impact by sector

isic	Industry	Rose effect	t-stat	Volatility	t-stat
40-41	electricity, gas and water supply	1.64	4.47	-15.78	-1.87
351	building and repairing of ships and boats	0.57	2.00	-15.87	-2.42
15-16	food products, beverages and tobacco	0.40	2.64	-7.78	-2.23
25	rubber and plastics products	0.35	2.25	-10.73	-3.04
35	other transport equipment	0.34	1.84	-17.72	-4.23
30	office, accounting and computing machinery	0.32	1.91	-5.77	-1.50
34	motor vehicles, trailers and semi-trailers	0.31	1.81	-13.78	-3.53
32	radio, television and communication equipment	0.27	1.68	-14.06	-3.74
36-37	manufacturing n.e.c.; recycling	0.27	1.76	-6.25	-1.76
353	aircraft and spacecraft	0.27	1.09	-16.89	-2.98
33	medical, precision and optical instruments	0.27	1.76	-7.75	-2.22
31	electrical machinery and apparatus, n.e.c.	0.26	1.64	-14.13	-3.94
28	fabricated metal products	0.25	1.66	-9.78	-2.85
17-19	textiles, textile products, leather and footwear	0.25	1.54	-12.00	-3.25
24	hemicals and chemical products	0.25	1.52	-8.80	-2.38
20	wood and products of wood and cork	0.23	1.41	-7.78	-2.08
29	machinery and equipment, n.e.c.	0.23	1.44	-9.29	-2.54
27	basic metals	0.19	1.16	-14.23	-3.70
26	other non-metallic mineral products	0.19	1.24	-10.29	-2.91
271+2731	iron and steel	0.14	0.74	-13.25	-3.08
2423	pharmaceuticals	0.13	0.70	-8.04	-1.90
272+2732	non-ferrous metals	0.12	0.63	-20.52	-4.72
01-05	agriculture, hunting, forestry and fishing	0.09	0.50	-7.59	-1.91
23	coke, refined petroleum products + nuclear fuel	0.03	0.12	-7.83	-1.33
352+359	railroad equipment + transport equipment n.e.c.	-0.05	-0.23	-14.09	-2.96
10-14	mining and quarrying	-0.21	-1.15	-9.84	-2.37

Source: Adapted from Baldwin et al. (2003).

4.1.4 Sectoral variation in the euro area Rose effect

While most studies of the euro's impact have focused on aggregate trade data, Taglioni (2002) and Baldwin et al. (2005) run the standard gravity model using sectoral data. In addition to confirming the general findings of the aggregate studies when all the sectors are pooled, this paper also provides sector-specific estimates of the Rose effect. The results are shown in Table 4.3.

What these results show is a rough correlation between the size of the Rose effect and what we loosely call ICIR sectors (imperfect competition and increasing return sectors). At the bottom of the list, we have agriculture as well as mining and quarrying, while near the top, we have various types of machinery and highly differentiated consumer goods such as food products, beverages and tobacco. This finding opens the door to the possibility that ICIR like effects – for example, the impact of uncertainty on market structure – may be part of the story.

The Flam-Nordström paper also provides sector results, which are reproduced in Table 4.4. These are broadly in line with the earlier estimates in Table 4.3. The sectors without a Rose effect tend to be those marked by fairly homogeneous products. Recall that trade inside Europe in agricultural goods is not free trade. Although there are no formal barriers, market intervention is pervasive.

As should be expected given the large number of studies reviewed, the collection of clues is far from cohesive. I turn now to introducing a framework that helps organize thinking on the causes of the Rose effect in the euro area.

4.2 Microeconomic changes that could produce a Rose effect

With the clues in hand it is time to twists the theories to fit the facts.

By my count, there are two channels through which the euro could have affected trade flows. I base this assertion on an uncontroversial theory, namely the demand function. Taking the destination nation's CES demand function for goods from the origin nation (nation-*o*):

$$
\begin{pmatrix} \text{Exports from} \\ \text{nation}o \text{ to d} \end{pmatrix} = \begin{pmatrix} \text{Number of nation}o \\ \text{varieties exported} \\ \text{to nation d} \end{pmatrix} \times \begin{pmatrix} \text{Relative price of} \\ \text{nation}o \text{ varieties} \\ \text{in nation d} \end{pmatrix}^{-\left(\substack{\text{import demand} \\ \text{elasticity}} \right)} \begin{pmatrix} \text{Nation d's real} \\ \text{expenditure} \end{pmatrix}
$$

Since we have fairly good data on real expenditure, the structural break in this demand equation – i.e. the Rose effect – must be coming through one of two channels:

- A change in the unobservable number-of-varieties variable.

- A change in the relative price that is not captured by the data included in the regressions.[38]

The relative price channel

The relative price has a numerator and a denominator. The numerator is the price of a typical nation-*o* variety in nation-*d*. The denominator is a price index of all competing varieties in nation-*d*'s market. As usual, we will measure all prices in the numeraire which we take here to be dollars.

Table 4.4 Flam-Nordström sectoral Rose effects

	SITC 1-9 Aggregate export	SITC 0 Food & live animals	SITC 1 Beverages & tobacco	SITC 2 Crude materials inedible, except fuels	SITC 3 Mineral fuels lubricants & related material	SITC 4 Animal & vegetable oils, fats & waxes	SITC 5 Chemincals & related products n.e.s.	SITC 6 Manufactured goods classified chiefly by materials	SITC 6 Machinery & transport equipment	SITC 8 Misc. manufactured articles
EMU11	0.172***	0.014	0.352***	-0.033	-0.196	0.044	0.069*	0.124***	0.224***	0.071***
	(0.021)	(0.041)	(0.086)	(0.054)	(0.198)	(0.152)	(0.038)	(0.034)	(0.037)	(0.027)
EMU12	0.089***	0.047	0.129*	-0.063	-0.096	0.186	0.078***	0.002	0.087**	-0.002
	(0.018)	(0.037)	(0.072)	(0.052)	(0.172)	(0.125)	(0.033)	(0.032)	(0.035)	(0.023)
EMU21	0.089***	-0.088**	0.161	-0.115***	0.075	0.139	0.059	0.088**	0.120***	0.009
	(0.019)	(0.0396)	(0.087)	(0.044)	(0.167)	(0.133)	(0.036)	(0.036)	(0.036)	(0.025)
ln(RYi)	0.864***	-0.990***	-0.693**	0.928***	-0.652	1.926**	1.955***	-0.661***	1.142***	0.160
	(0.125)	(0.243)	(0.303)	(0.328)	(0.910)	(0.907)	(.0250)	(0.167)	(0.131)	(0.159)
ln(RYj)	1.077***	0.868***	1.370***	0.574**	0.580	0.645	1.105***	0.735***	1.044***	0.608***
	(0.102)	(0.225)	(0.442)	(0.248)	(0.722)	(0.547)	(0.164)	(0.126)	(0.160)	(0.144)
ln(REXRij)	-0.811***	-1.610***	-1.695***	-1.268***	-2.459***	-1.934***	-1.180***	-1.262***	-0.805***	-1.302***
	(0.056)	(0.115)	(0.224)	(0.131)	(0.371)	(0.332)	(0.095)	(0.091)	(0.105)	(0.072)
ln(REXRcj)	0.380***	1.341***	1.373***	0.821***	1.608***	1.979***	0.886***	0.912***	0.178	0.887***
	(0.076)	(0.167)	(0.322)	(0.206)	(0.560)	(0.504)	(0.143)	(0.125)	(0.154)	(0.110)
nomexr	0.373	4.622***	6.232***	-2.371	-2.005	0.804	-2.754**	2.279**	0.026	4.655***
	(0.633)	(1.327)	(2.763)	(1.615)	(4.926)	(3.977)	(1.198)	(1.059)	(1.112)	(0.867)
obs	2704	2702	2659	2702	2536	2460	2703	2704	2704	2704
R2	0.994	0.985	.0961	0.975	0.914	0.917	0.987	0.991	0.988	0.993

Notes: Robust standard errors in parentheses. Significant at 10%; ** significant at 5%; *** significant at 1%.
Year, EU membership, 'Rotterdam effect' and bilateral (fixed effects) dummies included but not reported.
EMU11 = both nations in euro area (EA); EMU12 = origin nation in EA, destination nation not; EMU21 = destination nation in EA, origin nation not.

Turning first to the numerator, the price is related to the three terms in parentheses below, i.e. the bilateral mark-up, μ_{od}, the bilateral trade costs, τ_{od}, and nation-o's marginal production costs measured in dollars, μ_{co}. In symbols:

$$p_{od} = (\mu_{od})(\tau_{od})(mc_o)$$

This is true by definition, taking μ to be exactly the ratio of p_{od} to the domestic marginal production costs plus the bilateral trade costs.

The CES price index of all competing varieties will be the geometric average of the price of all competing varieties sold in nation-d, including those made in nation-d. That is:

$$P_d = \sum_i n_{id} (\mu_{id} \tau_{id} mc)^{1-\sigma}$$

The new varieties channel

Many varieties in nation-o are not exported to nation-d, a fact that has now been extensively documented in the so-called new-new trade theory (see Bernard et al., 2000). Notice that the n's enter the denominator of the relative price term, so the two channels are not mutually exclusive although a change in n_{od} will have a first-order large impact on bilateral trade, while changes in nation-i's n_{id} will affect o-to-d trade flows only indirectly.[39] In what follows, we turn to these channels one by one, considering the testable implications of each.

4.2.1　The relative price channel

Given the pass-through relationship and the definition of relative price, there are three ways in which the relative price channel could operate: a change in transaction costs (as measured by τ), a change in the mark-up (as measured by μ), or a change in the price index P_d. We consider each of these in turn and explain why each is inconsistent with the collection of clues summarized above.

Bilateral transaction costs: the Mundell story

In the traditional optimal currency area story, two nations that share the same money face lower transaction costs on bilateral trade and therefore trade more with each other. This is certainly the model that most Rose-effect researchers seem to have in the back of their minds when running their regressions.

I believe that the evidence completely rejects the standard transaction costs story and this on three separate counts. To make the case, we need to take the story seriously and work out what the theory tells us must be true in the data if the transaction cost story is right.

Implied transaction cost changes

Suppose the Rose effect on intra euro area is 10%. What would the reduction in bilateral transaction cost have to be if it was the main, indeed, the only change responsible for the Rose effect? The answer depends upon two elasticities and a share: the pass-through elasticity that determines what fraction of the transaction cost savings is passed on to consumers in the export market, the import demand elasticity in the importing nation, and the share of a euro area nation's expenditure that is affected by the changes. Totally differentiating the demand equation, we get:

$$\hat{X}_{od} = -\sigma(\hat{p}_{od}) + (\sigma - 1)\hat{P}_d \qquad (3)$$

Here the '^' symbol means proportional change. Under the maintained hypothesis that lower intra-EA transaction costs are the culprit, the bilateral τ should fall for all of nation-d's partners in the EA. This means that the price index change will be larger, the large is nation-d's share of expenditure on imports from the euro area. The precise formula is:

$$\hat{P}_d = share_{EZ}(\hat{p}_{od})$$

where $share_{EA}$ is share of expenditure in a typical EA member that falls on imports from other EA members. Leaning heavily on the assumption that transaction costs are driving the whole Rose effect, we see that the proportional change in the price will be the proportional change in the τ. The actual connection between the change in transaction costs and the landed price of imports will depend upon how much of the transaction cost reduction are passed on to foreign customers. Specifically,

$$\hat{p}_{od} = (PT \; elasticity \;)\hat{\tau}_{od}$$

where *PT* stands for 'pass through'. Empirically, the pass-though elasticity for exchange rate changes is much less than unity (Goldberg and Knetter, 1997), but there is an argument that a once-and-forever change in transaction cost would be passed through more fully. Combining all the steps, we get the implied connection between the transaction cost reduction and the trade volume change. It is:

$$\hat{X}_{od} = (\sigma(share_{EZ} - 1) - share_{EZ})(PT \; elasticity \;)\hat{\tau}_{od}$$

There are rough estimates as to the size of the transaction cost saving , for example European Commission (1990) puts it at 0.5% of GDP, but these are extremely crude and surely underestimate the total costs. Rather than trying to gauge the average savings, we reverse the deduction. We take 10% trade creation as data and ask how big the euro-induced drop transaction costs must have been to account for it.

To get an idea of what sort of transaction cost savings would be necessary, Table 4.5 solves for percent change in t that is implied by a 10% Rose effect under various assumptions on the demand elasticity (σ), the expenditure share and the pass-through elasticity. The left panel assumes full pass-through (of the transaction cost savings to trade prices) and then considers various combinations of import demand elasticities (down the leftmost column, ranging from 8 to 1) and EA-import expenditure shares (across the top of the panel, ranging from 0.5 to 0.1). For example, if the elasticity is very high at 8 and the import share is very low at 0.1, then the implied change in τ is only 1%. It is clear that the import demand elasticity is by far the most important parameter.

There is some dispute as to the true value of the import demand elasticity. At one extreme, Obstfeld and Rogoff (2000) assume, without empirical justification, that it is 8. Most empirical estimates yield an elasticity that is substantially lower. Gagnon (2003), for example, say his 'price elasticities for the most part are estimated close to -1, which is typical for the literature'. Elasticities above 4 are considered to be very high.

Taking a middle of the road estimate for the elasticity, say 2, and a 40% EA-imports expenditure share, the implied transaction cost reduction would have to be 6%. If there is less than full pass-through, the number has to be even higher.

It is important to note that this 6% transaction cost savings has to be on marginal costs, not average costs, since only marginal cost changes could get passed through to prices in the short run. Moreover, since the Rose effect seems to have appeared immediately, the transaction cost savings would have to be immediate, if it is the culprit. What sort of transaction costs could we be talking about? In the Mundellian tradition, the nature of these costs is usually left vague, but presumably they involve foreign exchange market commissions and some additional administrative costs for firms.

Table 4.5 Transaction cost drop (%) implied by a 10% Rose effect, various elasticities and shares

	Pass-through elasticity	1.0			Pass-through elasticity	0.5		
EA imports expenditure share:	0.5	0.4	0.2	0.1	0.5	0.4	0.2	0.1
Import demand elasticity:								
8	-2	-2	-2	-1	-4	-4	-3	-3
5	-3	-3	-2	-2	-7	-6	-5	-4
3	-5	-5	-4	-4	-10	-9	-8	-7
2	-7	-6	-6	-5	-13	-13	-11	-11
1	-10	-10	-10	-10	-20	-20	-20	-20

Source: Author's calculations.
Note: Percent figures rounded off by excel to the nearest 1%. The formula is: $d\tau/t = (\text{Rose effect})/\{(-\sigma + (\sigma-1)S)$ ´ PTelas\}, where S is the EA share and PTelas is the pass-through elasticity.

Problems with the bilateral transaction cost story

I believe there are three problems with transaction-cost savings of this magnitude.

- First, I find it hard to believe that corporations in Europe faced a marginal cost of 6% when switching between major European currencies. This admittedly is based on my priors and readers may or may not share them. The next two objections, however, are more scientific.

- Second, if transaction costs fell 6%, we should have seen a Rose effect in most sectors. Of course, since demand elasticities vary widely by sector, we can understand that there was some variation across sectors, but the Flam-Nordström and Baldwin-Taglioni results suggest that impact was concentrated in a few sectors. Flam-Nordström, for example, find a positive and statistically significant Rose effect in only four of the nine main categories of trade (SITC categories 0 to 8), and in two of the remaining five categories the effect is estimated as negative although not statistically significant.

- Third, the Rose effect appeared very quickly, in 1999 or even a year earlier, according to most studies. If the Mundellian story was responsible for this, the 6% transaction cost drop would have had to have been passed through to euro area trade prices quickly. This, in turn, means that we should have observed a structural break in the trade pricing equations and a sizeable one-off jump in euro area price convergence. As the literature reviewed in Chapter 2 showed, it appears that there has been some slow convergence, but definitely no jump in price convergence. Since such a price convergence jump is exactly what the transaction cost story asserts is behind the Rose effect, the failure to observe such a jump tells us that transactions costs were not the culprit, at least not in the early years of the monetary union.

Pricing transparency and the intra-EA mark-up

Pricing transparency is, after transaction costs, the most frequent hand-waving argument made for why we should believe that the euro could stimulate trade. The point is mentioned in the 1970 Werner report and echoed in the Commission's 1990 'One Market, One Money' report where the European Commission argued that 'without a completely transparent and sure rule of the law of one price for tradable goods and services, which only a single currency can provide, the single market cannot be expected to yield its full benefits – static and dynamic'. The Commission restated the argument in its 1996 Single Market Review, claiming 'increased price transparency will enhance competition and whet consumer appetites for foreign goods; price discrimination between different national markets (in the EU) will be reduced'. Translating their words into my organizing framework (the demand equation), the argument is that participation in the euro area could change the mark-up m in the above expressions.

A good way of thinking about the mark-up is as a measure of the degree of competition. The basic notion is that the euro promotes competition, which depresses price-cost mark-ups thus making imports cheaper. The net result is an increase in euro area imports. Since we do not have good data on the mark-ups, this sort of change would show up as a structural break in the gravity equation that is associated with usage of the euro (i.e. as a Rose effect).

Merits of the mark-up story

The mark-up change (implicitly due to a price-transparency-induced rise in competition) has many advantages over the transaction cost story.

The notion turns on a change in the markets of euro area nations – changes that make them extra good at importing (since import prices are depressed) without necessarily making them extra good at exporting. This means that the story is consistent with the 'clue' that the euro leads to no trade diversion.

Furthermore, the mark-up hypothesis is sufficiently flexible to account for the national and sector diversity in the Rose effect estimates. One could expect that the euro would increase competition among euro area companies, and indeed this is what many trade practitioners will tell you. However, it is quite likely that the effect would interact in a complex manner with various nation-specific and sector-specific features. For example, if the euro leads to greater price transparency for big-ticket items like cars and trucks, the impact would be very different in, say, Greece than it would be in Germany. The two nations differ greatly in terms of local producers and geographic distance to alternative suppliers. Likewise, the extent of the change in the mark-up could easily vary by sector. The obvious point is that the mark-up is pretty small already in some sectors and so unlikely to fall further. The more subtle point is that the pro-competitive effects of the euro could interact in complex ways with national regulations; a good example is banking. One would have thought that the elimination of currency risk would have allowed German homebuilders to get a mortgage in Luxembourg, but domestic regulations and practices effectively prevent this for now.

Problems with the mark-up story

The problem with the mark-up story stems for a feature it shares with the transaction-cost story – it implies a sudden convergence in euro area prices as the gap between local and export prices narrows. Moreover, if the mark-up is really the culprit, then the price convergence would have to be sudden and large since it has to account for a 10% increase in trade in the first years of monetary union. This, however, is inconsistent with one of the clues we discussed above, namely there does not seem to have been a sudden change in price dispersion. This is why I believe we can safely reject the pricing transparency story as the main culprit. Of course, many things in Europe changed at the same time and this 'crime' is unlikely to have a sole culprit, but we can say that the price transparency story could not have been a major cause since it does not fit with the pricing clues.

The price index route

The only possibility left in the relative price channel is a change in the importing nation's price index of competition goods. This route was discussed in a roundabout way by Micco et al. (2003b) and explicitly by Flam and Nordström (2003). Those authors noted that the euro's sharp depreciation would lower the price of intra-euro area trade (measured in dollars) relative to the price of competing goods from the dollar-zone. Since most versions of the gravity model do not explicitly control for exchange rates, such changes would show up as a structural break associated with the use of the use of the euro, i.e. as a Rose effect.

There are two problems with this story. First, Flam and Nordström (2003) do try to control for exchange rate changes and yet they still find a structural break that is roughly the size of the one found by other authors who do not control for exchange rates (or more precisely they control for bilateral exchanges by averaging the two uni-directional flows between each pair of nations). Second, the basic story requires the exports of non-EA nations to be extraordinarily expensive and thus extraordinarily low. This conflicts with the clue that non-EA nations seem to have experienced a positive Rose effect, i.e. the euro seems to have resulted in extraordinarily high exports from non-EA members. Indeed, in the Flam-Nordström results that include the USA and Japan, the increase in non-EA exports to the EA due to the euro's introduction is even larger.

This leads me to reject the price index route as the main suspect. With this route eliminated, we have eliminated all possible routes in the relative price channel.

4.2.2 New goods – the extensive margin story

> Holmes to Watson: 'How often have I said to you that when you have eliminated the impossible, whatever remains, however impossible, must be the truth?' (*The Sign of Four*)

A fascinating paper by Andrew Bernard and Brad Jensen decomposes the growth of US exports in the 1990s into an intensive margin, i.e. an increase in the volume of goods that were already exported, and an extensive margin, i.e. an increase due to newly exported goods. The paper, Bernard and Jensen (2004), used data from individual plants for the entire US manufacturing to establish this breakdown. The really new finding was that a non-negligible share came from firms that switched between only selling locally to selling locally and abroad. This brought to centre stage the little known fact that most firms in most nations do not export even when they are in so-called traded goods sectors; they produce only for the local market, often selling to other firms.

The relevance of this work here is to alert us to the fact that the Rose effect might have happened due to a change in the number of varieties each nation exports. There are many things to recommend this idea.

- First, since it involves existing firms selling existing varieties in new markets, it could happen quite quickly.

- Second, the size of the effect could vary quite a lot across sectors since market structures vary so much. For example, the Flam-Nordström results suggest that the Rose effect was systematically large in sectors such as chemicals and transport equipment where scale economies and imperfect competition are important, but the effect was small in other sectors.

- Third, the size of the effect could vary a great deal across euro area nations since the decision to introduce new varieties is constrained by all sorts of legal barriers and implicit market arrangements.

- Fourth, the effect could happen without any convergence in prices. Indeed, all the explanations that work via the relative price term should have also shown up as structural breaks in the pricing equation. But even the most casual glance at the demand reveals that the number of exported varieties does not enter the pricing equation. A 'structural break' in 'n' would thus create a structural break in the trade volume equation without creating one in the trade price equation.

- Fifth, it could happen without generating trade diversion, if euro usage implied a lower cost of entry into euro area markets.

Melitz model and newly exported goods

Until very recently, mainstream international economics ignored the fact that trade barriers could affect the number of goods one nation exports to another. One influential paper that has helped change this is Melitz (2003). The model has much in common with early trade models such as those by Paul Krugman and Elhanan Helpman (1985), but there are two key innovations that add complexity in both the good and bad sense of the word. Since I believe that the introduction of new goods is the key to explaining the Rose effect in Europe, it is worth spending some space developing intuition for these models, the so-called new-new trade theory. We start, however, with its precedent – the new trade theory.

Determination of the number of goods produced in the 'new' trade theory

The two new elements in the new-new trade theory are: (1) fixed cost of entering a new market; and (2) differences in firm's marginal production costs. These are combined with the standard elements of the Helpman-Krugman trade model, which is often called the new trade theory although it is more than 25 years old. To fix ideas, we work out the determination of the number of goods without the two extra elements.

In the new trade theory, firms produced differentiated varieties that compete indirectly with each other via monopolistic competition. That is to say, each firm makes a unique variety and it has a monopoly on this, but its market power is limited to the residual demand curve, namely the demand that is left over after other firms have sold their goods. Firms face increasing returns to scale, so they must sell at least a given amount to cover costs. Due to this breakeven constraint, the number of firms is determined in the market; however, in the new trade theory the number of varieties a given nation produces is fixed by the nation's supply of productive factors. Big nations (i.e. nations with lots of productive factors) will produce a wider range of goods than small nations.

A very insightful way of thinking about the determination of the number of goods produced is to think of firms entering until the residual demand curve facing a typical firm has been driven down (or back) to the point where all firms just break even. This is illustrated in Figure 4.4.

In the model of imperfect competition used most frequently in the new trade theory (the Dixit-Stiglitz model), firms always find it profit-maximizing to charge a price that is a constant mark-up on their marginal costs. For convenience, the marginal cost of all firms is assumed to be the same, namely MC in the diagram. Combining these two points we see immediately that a firm's profitability depends only upon how much it sells. If it faces few competitors, the residual demand curve will be far to the right, e.g. RD3 in the diagram, so it will sell a lot and thus earn high operating profits (i.e. profits before we subtract off fixed costs); in the diagram the operating profit equals areas A+B+C. If A+B+C is more than the firm needs to cover its fixed costs, the typical firm will earn pure profits. This state of affairs will attract new entrants so the residual demand facing a typical firm shifts inward, say to RD2, and operating profit drops to A+B. This process of introducing new goods goes on until the operating profit of the typical firm is just sufficient to cover fixed costs associated with production. Now turning this around, we see that every firm will, in equilibrium, be of the same size in terms of sales. And this, in turn, means that big nations will produce many varieties compared to small nations.

The problem is more complex when firms sell in multiple markets since the true marginal cost of selling in a foreign market must include the bilateral trade costs. As a consequence, firms have different levels of prices and sales in each market. The breakeven condition is that they make sufficient operating profits in all markets to cover their fixed cost associated with production. This equilibrium is not easy to show graphically (so I do not) but the logic extends easily to many markets with a bit of mathematics. The conclusion is the same; big markets produce lots of varieties and all of them are sold to all markets. This last point means that we cannot use the new trade theory to explain a jump in the number of traded varieties. We need the new-new trade theory.

Figure 4.4 Determining the number of goods in a 'new trade' model

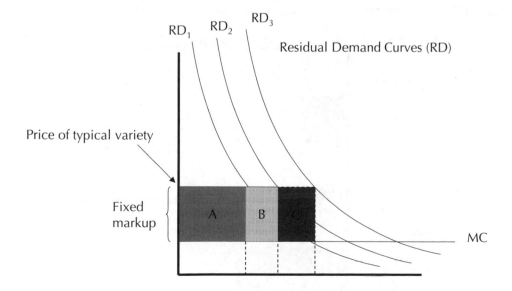

Determination of the number of goods produced in the 'new-new' trade theory

The new-new trade theory focuses on heterogeneous firms, in particular on differences in firm-level efficiency and therefore firm-level marginal costs. To see how this changes things, consider a diagram similar to Figure 4.4 but where firms have different marginal costs.

To keep things simple, we assume that all varieties are viewed as equally good by consumers, so they all face the same residual demand function. The heterogeneity only comes through marginal costs. Starting with a given residual demand curve, we can show how operating profits vary for firms with different marginal costs in Figure 4.5.

The diagram shows three firms with progressively higher marginal costs, MC_1, MC_2 and MC_3. Following the profit-maximizing fixed mark-up pricing rule, the firms charge progressively higher prices and thus sell progressively less; the small firm (as measured by sales) is the high marginal-cost firm. We also see that they earn progressively lower operating profits: areas A, B and C.

In a closed economy this sort of reasoning will give us a 'threshold MC' – firms with marginal costs above some threshold will not find it worthwhile to produce. This concept is quite intuitive and indeed it will suffice for extrapolating to the open economy case that we are really interested in, but it is important to note that this glosses over the major technical difficulties of the Melitz model – the position of the residual demand curve. In fact, the residual demand depends upon the number of active firms (for the reasons discussed in Figure 4.4) and upon the distribution of their marginal costs (if many firms have low marginal costs, they will sell a lot and then the residual demand curve will be shifted inwards a lot). Thus we must simultaneously solve for the number of firms and the threshold marginal cost. This is the source of most of the Melitz model's mathematical difficulties. Fortunately, the basic intuition we get from a fixed RD curve goes through even with more complete reasoning if we assume that the RD in Figure 4.5 is in its equilibrium position.

Figure 4.5 Determining the range of goods in a 'new new' trade model

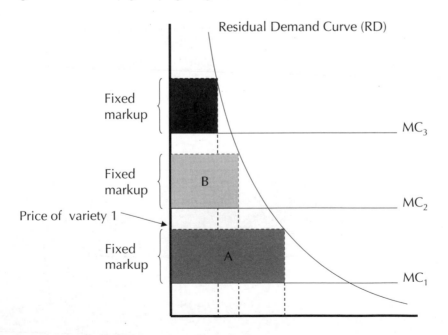

With all this background firmly in hand, the basic economic logic of the determination of the number of traded goods is simple to portray. The key question is: 'If a firm is already covering its fixed production costs in its local market, will it also export its goods to all other nations in the world?'

To address this question, we have to be specific about what separates the local and export markets, i.e. trade costs. It is natural to suppose that there are per-unit trade costs – the usual costs related to distance and manmade trade barrier that raise the cost by, say, 10% per unit shipped. (In the discussion of the gravity model, I denoted the marginal trade costs as t.) As mentioned above, a key extra assumption in the Melitz model is that firms face a fixed cost per market. For example, to sell in a new market, a firm has to invest something in establishing the brand name (if it is a consumer product), or establishing contacts with purchasers (if it is an intermediate product). There are also fixed costs related to product regulations. Most relevant to the case at hand is the fixed costs of managing an extra currency; these could involve bank charges, additional staff, more complex accounting procedures, etc.

Using the Figure 4.5 reasoning as an analogy, it is clear that only firms with sufficiently low marginal costs will be able to sell to foreign markets, since only they will be able to cover the fixed market-entry costs (due to the fixed mark-up rule, they fully pass on the per-unit trade costs to foreign customers so the price of their good will be higher in foreign markets). In other words, we will get a second threshold – the export threshold – that determines which domestically produced goods are exported.

This threshold implies that the model's predictions are in line with the common observation that big, efficient firms are more likely to export than small firms. Moreover, the further away is the market, the higher will be the price (due to passed-through trade costs) and so the lower will be the operating profit earned. This means that firms with a given marginal cost may find it worth their while to pay market-entry costs in nearby markets, but not in distant markets. In other words, the export threshold for marginal costs is lower for more distant markets.

The final step is to connect the export threshold and the number of goods exported. As the threshold marginal cost rises, smaller firms will export their goods, so the range of exported goods will widen. For completeness sake, note that with two nations the model is analytically solvable but with more nations it can be worked out with paper and pencil only under highly restrictive assumptions. It can be solved numerically for general cases, and indeed Rocha (2006) shows that lower one nation's market-entry cost can lead to a Rose effect without trade diversion.

The euro's impact

Finally, we are ready for the heart of the matter – the impact of introducing the euro on the number of goods exported. Assume that the introduction of the euro lowers the fixed market entry costs in euro area nations. One very concrete story would be that the fixed costs associated with managing an extra currency are lower for the euro, which has a large, deep market, than it was for the legacy currencies. Importantly, the assumption is that the fixed cost falls for all exporters to the euro area, not just for firms that are located inside the euro area. For example, a Swedish firm that wanted to sell to all 12 euro area nations had to deal with 11 currencies before 1999 (Belgium and Luxembourg have had a currency union since the 1950s), but afterwards it had to deal with only one. Under this story, it is plausible that the drop in fixed cost would be greater for EA-based firms than for non-EA-based firms. For firms located inside the euro area, all fixed costs related to foreign exchange in the euro area disappear since after 1999 the local and export currencies are the same.

If the fixed cost of entering the euro area markets falls, then a wider range of firms will find selling to the euro area to be worthwhile. As a consequence, the number of goods exported to the euro area will increase, both from the euro area nations and from non-euro area nations. More goods, in turn, mean a higher trade volume. Note that this simultaneously accounts for the positive Rose effect within the euro area and the lack of trade diversion.

Note that this story is flexible enough to account for sector variation and nation-specific variation. In particular, the Melitz model works in industries marked by imperfect competition and increasing returns, but not in commodity-like sectors – just the pattern that the sector studies suggest. The key difference is that in commodity-like sectors, say 'Food and live animals', or 'Crude materials', the market structure is not dominated by individual firms selling differentiated goods. Moreover, even among differentiated-goods sectors, the distribution of firm-size can alter the industry's response to a given change in the fixed costs. Observe that it is also flexible enough to allow for geographic variation if one supposes that foreign-exchange-linked market entry costs were affected in different ways in different euro area members, and that the firm-size distribution is different in different nations.

As far as I know, there are only two formal model of the new goods hypothesis. Baldwin and Taglioni (2004) present a formal model of the Rose effect of this which has the additional element of exchange rate uncertainty. The basic intuition is simple. Most European firms are not engaged in trade; they sell only in their local markets due to a variety of reasons – one of which is aversion to exchange rate uncertainty. Such uncertainty is a nuisance to giant companies like Nestlé and Fiat, but to small and medium firms it is a very real barrier. The story is that monetary union eliminated this uncertainty and thus increased the number of firms in the euro area that are engaged in exporting to other euro area markets. A sudden and permanent reduction of bilateral volatility within the euro area thus led to an increase in exports with little change in the basic production structure. This story rests on the Melitz model (Melitz, 2003) where the range of firms that export is endogenously determined and related to native firm-level productivity so that large firms export while small firms do not. Rocha (2006) is the other formal model; it focuses on the three-country case and thus can account for the lack of trade diversion (Baldwin-Taglioni works with only two nations).

Do the facts fit?

> Inspector Gregory: "Is there any other point to which you would wish to draw my attention?"
> Holmes: 'To the curious incident of the dog in the night-time"
> "The dog did nothing in the night time"
> "That was the curious incident", remarked Sherlock Holmes.
> (from *The Adventure of Silver Blaze* by Arthur Conan Doyle)

Consider the clues that Sherlock would have before him. The effect happened very quickly, far too quickly for the new trade to be explained by important changes in production structures. Moreover, given the very small size of the likely transaction cost reductions entailed in monetary union (even smaller than the one linked to currency union), the size of the effect seems to be too large to be explained by a drop in transaction costs. The keystone clue is that pricing in post-euro Europe did not experience a sudden break at the time the trade flows jumped up. Since the trade volume jumped suddenly, the lack of a jump in the trade pricing behaviour is indeed some 'other point to which you would wish to draw my attention'. The lack of a break in the pricing equations is the dog that did not bark.

I believe that the only story that is consistent with all the clues is the new-good hypothesis. The next chapter considers some direct evidence that is supportive of this deduction.

5　Testing the New-Goods Hypothesis

> There are three principal means of acquiring knowledge...observation of nature, reflection, and experimentation. Observation collects facts; reflection combines them; experimentation verifies the result of that combination. (Denis Diderot)

I formulated the new-goods hypothesis in the last chapter as a way of accounting for all the clues in the existing empirical literature. This chapter takes things one step further. If new goods are indeed the 'culprit', then we should be able to find direct evidence of their introduction. In particular, the number of goods exported to euro area markets should have increased by more than the number of goods exported to EU-but-non-euro area markets. This chapter investigates whether this prediction holds for European nations. (This chapter is based on joint work with my graduate student Virginia Di Nino, in particular on Baldwin and Di Nino, 2006).

An example

To fix ideas, it is useful to give a fictitious but illustrative example of how the euro could stimulate trade in new goods. In 1997, a Swiss company sold a highly specialised global positioning system (GPS) unit for runners in the German market, but not in the Austrian market. The reason was that although they could sell a few units in Austria at their standard retail price, the number was too low to justify the cost of entering the Austrian market. Part of these fixed costs involved the separate currency. For example, the Swiss company would have to set up a bank account in Vienna and some sort of hedging operation as well as work out a way to convert the shilling sales into its Swiss franc-based accounting system. And of course, they would need to pay an employee to keep an eye on all this new financial activity in Vienna. They did all these things for the German market, but that was sensible since 80 million potential customers used deutschmarks. In 1999, the German banking/hedging/accounting/supervision operation was converted to euros. This lowered the extra fixed cost of entering the Austrian market, so the Swiss company started shipping to sports stores in Austria and another zero dropped out of the Swiss export vector to Austria.

I could tell the same story for a small German firm that initially only sold in Germany but started exporting to euro-using nations after 1999. Importantly, this story suggest that the stimulation to new goods could be greater for euro area-based nations than it is for nations, like the Swiss GPS firm, that do not use the euro at home. In the example, the impact on Swiss exports applies only to Swiss firms that were already exporting to one euro area market already (and perhaps some Swiss firms that were almost efficient enough to export). For Germany, the reduced currency-related fixed cost savings would apply to every German-based firm from the smallest to the largest. By this mechanism, it is possible that the euro's introduction would increase the number of new products exported to Austria from both Switzerland and Germany, but more from Germany.

Dataset problems

The ideal dataset would be to have partner-specific export data by firm. Unfortunately such data are not available to researchers. As a fall back strategy, we use the finest level of dis-aggregation in the publicly available trade data, namely the six-digit level of the Harmonized System (HS) from Comtrade database. We have the data for the 1990-2003, but generally only use the post-1993 data to avoid problems with the switch in collection methodology. The set of countries encompasses the EU15 (actually only 14 since Belgium's and Luxembourg's trade data are fused at this level of dis-aggregation) and three non-EU nations in Europe: Switzerland, Norway and Iceland.

This dataset is enormous. For most of our 17 exporters there are about 5,000 product categories for each partner, i.e. about 85,000 data points per year per exporter. Since we are looking for changes around the euro's introduction we use 1993-98 as the 'before' period and 1999-2003 as the 'after' period. This means 11 years in all, so the dataset is of the order of a million data points for each exporting nation. Pooling all 17 exporters together would create a panel of about 16 million data points, a number which defies our computational capacity. To get around this computation problem, only one exporter's data is used at a time.

Keep in mind that the six-digit classification is not fine enough to pick up individual products. As a consequence, looking for changes in the number of zeros will systematically underestimate the importance of new goods. That is, there may be many new goods traded that we cannot pick up since they occur in categories where trade is already occurring. The only new goods we can observe directly are those in categories that switch from zero value to some positive value during our data period (there are very few switches from positive values to zero, so we work with the total number of zeros).

The only control variable is gross domestic product, more precisely the current US dollar GDP, which is extracted from the World Development Indicators (World Bank). The effect of distance, the other standard control variable in gravity estimations is, in the specific case, already accounted for in the partner dummies.

5.1 First look at the data

Before turning to more formal statistical tests, we look for prima facie evidence on the new-goods hypothesis.

5.1.1 Evolution of zeros for Germany

Figure 5.1 shows the evolution of the number of categories that are zero for any give bilateral relationship for Germany. Before discussing the graphs, it is important to be precise about what the numbers are measuring.

The six-digit HS system listed 5,020 products in 2003, but the number has increased somewhat over the years as new six-digit categories were created to reflect new products. Moreover, there are some HS-6 categories where Germany never exported, so these are not in our dataset.[40] Thus the total universe of products in our dataset includes all products for which the nation has exported something to someone during 1990-2003. For Germany, there are 4,823 categories which have positive values for at least one year with at least one partner.

Figure 5.1 Evolution of zeros for Germany's exports to EU15 nations, 1990-2003

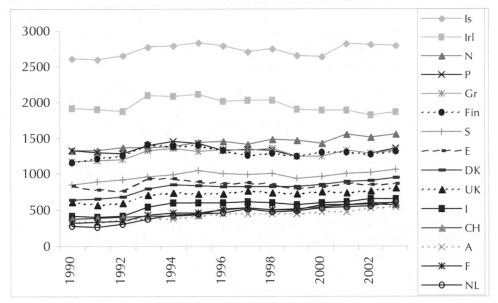

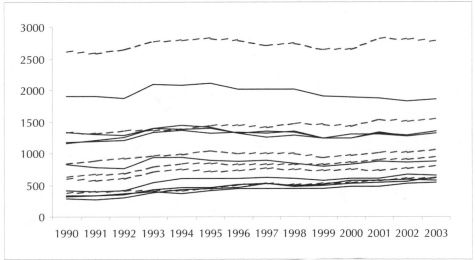

Cross-sectional variation

We start by looking at the cross-sectional (i.e. by partner) variation for Germany in the top panel of Figure 5.1. What we see is that the difference in the number of zeros varies far more by partner than it does over time. The diagram shows that – as predicted by the Melitz model – there is a rough correlation between the level of zeros by partner and the distance between the exporting and importing market. Ireland, Iceland and Norway are top three countries for zeros; the lowest number of zeros are with the Netherlands and Austria.

Time-series variation

Figure 5.1 shows that the number of zeros has been rising over time for almost all German partners. Part of this is an accounting illusion. The Harmonized System has created more categories over time and this automatically creates more zeros. For example, if all German cars were lumped into a single category, there would be very few bilateral zeros – although Germany does not export every model to every nation, it exports some cars to everyone. If the Harmonized system becomes finer over time – distinguishing, for example, between small cars and luxury cars – our data would automatically show a rise in the number of zeros even if there were no change in exports.

The top panel of Figure 5.1 identifies the individual partners, but the number of partners makes it difficult to discern a clear pattern. The bottom panel shows the EA partners with solid lines and the non-EA partners with dashed lines. There are two salient points:

- Using our method of (under)estimating the impact of the euro on zeros, the impact is very subtle – there is no clear jump down in the number of zeros for Germany's exports to its euro area partners.

- A sufficiently generous observer could detect a slightly larger increase in the number of zeros in Germany's exports to non-euro nations than in its exports to euro nations. This is confirmed by more statistical analysis below, but from this example we see that the impact is rather subtle.

Figure 5.2 Sum of zeros for EA nations, non-EA EU nations and non-EU nations

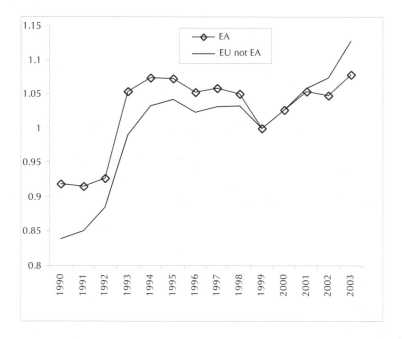

Figure 5.2 shows one way to study this point more clearly. The Figure plots an index (base year 1999 = 1.0) of the zeros for the euro area 'ins', and the three EU15 nations that do not use the euro. The first thing to note is that all intra-EU partners experienced a sharp increase in zeros in 1993. This was probably due to the switch in trade data collection methods. From 1993, intra-EU trade data was gathered from value-added tax statistics instead of customs data, while non-EU trade data continued to be based on customs data. Since filling out VAT reimbursement forms involves

some administrative costs, it is likely that quite a number of small intra-EU trade flows switched from reported to unreported in 1993 (recall that Sweden, Finland and Austria joined in 1994 and so their trade flows switched reporting systems in 1994 rather than 1993).

In the post-1999 period, it seems that the number of zeros on intra-EA trade stayed approximately flat overall (with an important dip in 1999) while the zeros in non-EA partners rose, especially after 1999.

So far we have limited the analysis to the number of zeros, but it interesting to see the value of trade generated by goods that switched from non-traded to traded. A couple of simple statistics serves the purpose. In Germany, international trade increased by 22% between 1999 and 2003; 2% of this was due to trade in 'new goods' (the quasi-extensive margin – quasi since we cannot pick of new goods in categories that were already traded) and a remaining 20% is the quasi-intensive margin (again, quasi since there is some mixing of new goods and more of old goods). As noted, this measure of new goods is probably an underestimate since we can only pick up new goods where no goods were traded before. These figures provide clear testimony to the importance of the extensive margin in European trade.

5.1.2 Evolution of zeros: group averages

Germany is Europe's largest trader by far and it is also the nation for whom one might think that the euro had the least impact (most European nations were de facto pegged to the deutschmark even before 1999). Reproducing Figure 5.2 for the other 16 exporters in our sample would take up too much space, so we plot the averages for various groups of exporters in Figure 5.3.

Figure 5.3 Sum of zeros to EA nations from three groups of exporters (EA, EU not EA and non-EU)

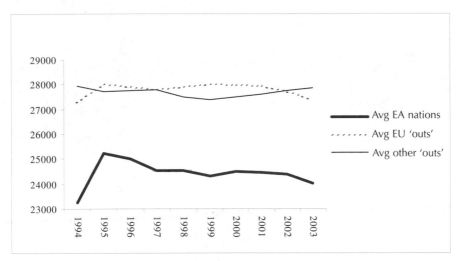

Three groups of exporters naturally suggest themselves: the euro area group, the EU15 nations that did not adopt the euro (UK, Sweden and Denmark), and the non-EU nations Switzerland, Norway and Iceland (who obviously did not adopt the euro since EU membership is a requirement for euro area membership). We are interested in seeing whether the euro had an impact independent of other EU integration initiatives (recall that the Single Market is being deepened continuously in the post-

1986 period); we look at the number of zeros in exports to EU 'ins' versus EU 'outs'. This leads us to look at the three group averages for number zeros in their exports to the euro area markets. That is, we sum the number of zeros in each exporter's sales to all the euro area nations, then we take the average number for each of our groups. For example, the average for the three outsiders (Norway, Switzerland and Iceland) in 1999 is the average number of zeros in Norwegian, Swiss and Icelandic exports to the euro area nations; the average is roughly 28,000 zeros to all 11 EA markets (taking Belgium and Luxembourg as one).[41]

Figure 5.3 shows the results. For the euro area group (marked Avg EA nations) we see a gradual drop in the number of zeros into the euro area. The dotted line (marked Avg EU3 'outs') shows the average for the three EU 'outs', i.e. nations that are members of the EU15 – and thus members of the Single Market – but not members of the euro area. The thin solid line (marked Avg Other 'outs') shows the average number of zeros in the three's exports to the euro area. The main point to take away from the graph is that the Single Market seems to matter independently of the euro. The two averages for EU nations show a marked increase in new goods sold to the euro area, but the average for the non-EU nations does not. From the contrast between the EU 'outs' and the non-EU 'outs' we can guess that the Single Market programme has been reducing zeros totally independently of the euro's impact.

Now that we know that the Single Market matters, we shall have to control for it by considering only exporters that are located in the Single Market, i.e. EU exporters. To isolate the impact of the euro on the exports of new goods, we want to see if the number of zeros dropped more for exports to the euro area markets than it did to non-euro area EU markets (limiting ourselves to EU exporters)

Figure 5.4 Ratio of zeros to EA and non-EA destinations inside the EU, 'ins' versus the 'outs'

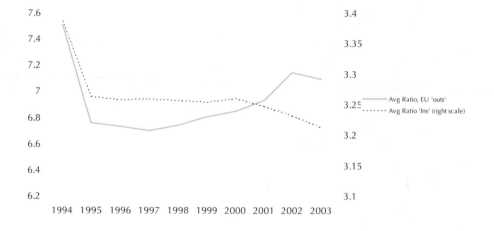

To make it easy to detect the euro's impact we take the ratio of zeros to EA and non-EA markets. Specifically, for each exporting nation we take the ratio of its zeros to the euro area markets and its zeros to the non-EA EU markets. Then, as before, we form group averages, one for nations that are inside the euro area and one for the three EU 'outs'. Before turning to the numbers, consider what the new-goods hypothesis would predict. The new-goods hypothesis claims that euro-usage in the destination market somehow lowers the fixed market entry cost for all firms exporting to that destination market, so the number of zeros in export vectors to euro-using nations should fall. There is, by contrast, no change in the fixed cost of entering non-euro destination markets so there should be no drop in the number of zeros to non-euro markets. The ratio of the former to the latter should therefore fall. Furthermore, since firms based in the euro area are automatically using the euro, it is possible that the impact would be greatest on EA to EA trade flows.

Figure 5.4 shows the plot of the two group-averages. We see that both the EU 'ins' (i.e. the euro area nations) and the EU 'outs' (UK, Sweden and Denmark) experienced a sharp drop in the ratio of zeros in 1995. This seems to be due to the 1994 enlargement of the EU. After 1995, the ratio of the 'outs' (marked by Avg Ratio, EU 'outs') has risen more or less steadily. The ratio of the 'ins', by contrast, has fallen, with some hint of an acceleration after the euro's introduction. Note that the two lines are plotted on different y-axes.

This graph is not proof by any means. Many things affect the number of zeros and these other confounding factors are not controlled for in the graph. But it does suggest that the new-goods hypothesis cannot be rejected out of hand. Exporters based in the euro area saw a drop in export zeros to the EU 'ins' compared to the export zeros to EU 'outs'. For exporters based in non-euro-using markets, the ratio rose. Something must have caused this difference in differences, but we cannot be quite sure that it was the euro's introduction. For example, it could have been due to differential growth in the 'ins' and 'outs' markets. In short, we must control for other factors.

Undertaking these controls requires more formal statistical procedures.

5.2 Statistical estimates

The decision to export a particular good to a particular nation is complex. In particular, it is easy to think that the decision would turn on a trade-off between the amount that could be sold and the costs of doing so. Plainly both trade costs and market size would affect sales (as in the gravity model), so these are things we will have to control for when looking for a Rose effect on the extensive margin.

5.2.1 Estimating the total Rose effect: Tobit regressions

Before focusing tightly on the new-goods hypothesis, we use our highly disaggregated datasets to estimate overall Rose effects. As we shall see, our findings are not too different from those in the literature that uses aggregate trade flows.

The estimating equation is the basic gravity model discussed in Chapter 2. Namely:

$$V_{od} = \left(\tau_{od}\right)^{1-elasticity} \frac{Y_o}{\Omega_o} \frac{E_d}{P_d^{1-elasticity}};$$

where V_{od} is the dollar value of exports from nation-o to nation-d. We measure E_d (expenditure in the importing nation) with the dollar value nation-d's GDP. We include time dummies to deal with the conversion of all the current valued dollars to a common base year. Since we have a single exporting nation in each dataset (there are 17 datasets), the time dummy also picks up the impact of the origin nation's Y and Ω, so we exclude these from the regression.[42] To adjust for the nation-d price index, P_d, we included a Partner dummy in each regression. Since there is a single exporting nation, the Partner dummies act exactly like pair dummies.

When dealing with highly disaggregated data, the issue of zero trade flows cannot be ignored. Indeed, the fact that many product categories switch from zero to positive values is an important part of our stories so we use Tobit estimation rather than OLS. The results for the period 1993-2003 are shown in Table 5.1.

Table 5.1 Tobit estimates: the overall Rose effect

Exporter	Euro dummy coefficient	Standard error	p-value
Austria	0.16***	0.0253	0.00
Spain	0.25***	0.0332	0.00
France	0.10***	0.0183	0.00
Ireland	0.29***	0.0473	0.00
Netherlands	-0.12***	0.0198	0.00
Portugal	0.28***	0.0369	0.00
Finland	0.05***	0.0175	0.00
Belgium-Luxembourg	0.06***	0.0219	0.01
Italy	0.04**	0.0190	0.04
Germany	0,05**	0.0255	0.05
Greece	-0.03	0.0459	0.59
Raw Avg	0.10		
UK	0.10***	0.0164	0.00
Denmark	0.04*	0.0218	0.09
Sweden	0.04*	0.0240	0.07
Raw Avg	0.06		
Switzerland	0.12***	0.0227	0.00
Iceland	-0.36***	0.1051	0.00
Norway	0.17***	0.0277	0.00
Raw Avg	-0.02		

Notes: Significantly different from zero at ***1% level, ** 5% level, and *10% level. The estimated equation is:

$$\ln V_{od,i} = c + \beta(EuroDummy_{od}) + \gamma \ln(GDP_d) + time\ dummies + partner\ dummies$$

where i is the product category index for each six-digit category. The EuroDummy is unity from 1999 onward for destination nation in the euro area (2001 for Greece). When the EuroDummy coefficient is near zero, the raw coefficient gives a good approximation of the % boost in trade since the exp(ε)-1≈ε when ε is near zero. The partner nations in all datasets are the 14 EU nations (Belgium and Luxembourg's data are fused), Switzerland, Iceland and Norway; the exporting nation is dropped from the list of partners in each regression. The bilateral trade data is taken from the exporting nation (called the 'reporter' in ComTrade jargon). The GDP coefficients are given in the Appendix to this chapter. The number of observations varies according to the exporting nation, but is over 400,000 in all cases.

The results are generally in line with what has been found in aggregate estimates of the euro area Rose effect. This should not be surprising since most researchers have worked with aggregate trade data which is just the sum of all our disaggregated data. In particular, the unweighted average of the euro area coefficients for euro area nations implies a Rose effect of about 10%, which is very much in line with the literature. Two remarks on the euro-using nations are in order.

- We find that Greece's coefficient is negative, although not statistically different from zero (MSO (2003) also find that Greece's effect is negative but insignificant). This may be due to the very short period of Greek membership in the euro area, or it may reflect real factors that we do not account for in the model. Note, however, that since the data involve only Greek exports, the equation allows for a Greek-specific constant, time-dummies and partner dummies, so any time invariant features of Greece's trade relations with its 16 partners are controlled for.

- We also find that the Rose effect on Dutch export data is negative and significantly different from zero. We believe that this is due to the so-called Rotterdam effect and policies intended to combat VAT fraud that were described at length in Chapter 3.

The second set of results, for the nations that are EU members but not in the euro group, show that the euro boosted exports of outsiders as well. The unweighted average suggests the Rose effect was about 6% (i.e. the exports of EU but not euro-using nations to euro area nations rose by about 6% when the single currency was introduced). Again, this is in line with existing estimates on aggregate trade flows. For example, Flam and Nordström (2003) report the number to be approximately 7%. Interestingly, the figure for Britain is as big as the number for France, but the numbers for Denmark and Sweden are much smaller.

The third set of results is for the European nations that are outside the EU and thus outside the euro area. Here the results for Switzerland and Norway are quite similar to those for Britain, namely, their exports to euro area members rose by about 10% or so. The negative and significant result for Iceland is hard to interpret due to Iceland's unusual export mix (fish 71% and aluminium 13%).

We believe that these results suggest that the basic gravity model specification we are using and our dataset provide reasonable results. This noted, we now turn our attention to the extensive margin.

5.2.2 Binary models: an underestimate of the new-good effect

To investigate the role of the euro in creating trade in new categories, we estimate the probability of observing a positive trade flow in a particular category. The equation estimated is the same as in the previous section, but since we are estimating the probability of positive trade, the left-hand side variable is a zero-one variable that is one if there was some trade in the six-digit category in a given year and zero otherwise. As before, we include time dummies and partner dummies. Since there is a single exporter in each dataset, the partner dummies wipe out all time-invariant cross-section variation. This means that the coefficients are estimated of the time-variation of the zero-one left-hand variable. In plain English, we are estimating the impact of the euro on the likelihood of trade appearing in a new category. As discussed above, this is an underestimate of the role of new-goods since we cannot pick up the entry of new goods in categories where some trade is already going on.

The results in Table 5.2 provide direct evidence in support of the new-goods hypothesis. Since the left-hand side variable is the zero-one variable indicating positive trade, the coefficient on EuroDummy can be interpreted as the probability by which euro-usage increases the chance of observing trade in a given category. Of course, there may be many new goods appearing in previously traded categories that this regression does not pick up. We can be sure, however, that a switch from zero to positive involves new goods. Thus the positive coefficients indicate that euro-usage promotes the likelihood of new goods being traded.

More specifically, all the point estimates are positive except those for Dutch and Icelandic exports (two nations whose particular situations were discussed above). Seven of the 15 positive coefficients are statistically significant at the 1% level or better; nine at the 10% level or better. We take this as supportive but far from conclusive evidence that the euro promotes the exports of new goods.

Table 5.2 Impact of the Euro on promoting trade in new categories: logit regressions

Exporter	Euro dummy coefficient	Standard error	p-value
Austria	0.05***	0.0100	0.00
Spain	0.08***	0.0108	0.00
France	0.02*	0.0096	0.06
Ireland	0.09***	0.0136	0.00
Netherlands	-0.08***	0.0090	0.00
Portugal	0.08***	0.0117	0.00
Finland	0.01	0.0107	0.44
Belgium-Luxembourg	0.02*	0.0102	0.10
Italy	0.00	0.0101	0.64
Germany	0.01	0.0096	0.35
Greece	0.02	0.0167	0.34
Raw Avg	0.03		
UK	0.04***	0.0109	0.00
Denmark	0.01	0.0094	0.18
Sweden	0.01	0.0097	0.42
Raw Avg	0.02		
Switzerland	0.05***	0.0098	0.00
Iceland	-0.09***	0.0334	0.01
Norway	0.07***	0.0109	0.00
Raw Avg	0.01		

Notes: Significantly different from zero at ***1% level, ** 5% level, and *10% level.
The estimated equation is:
where $D_{od,i}$ is the zero-one indicator of whether there is a positive value of bilateral trade in the given category

$$D_{od,i} = c + \beta(EuroDummy_{od}) + \gamma \ln(GDP_d) + time\ dummies + partner\ dummies$$

in the given year.
The EuroDummy is unity from 1999 onward for destination nation in the euro area (2001 for Greece). When the EuroDummy coefficient is near zero, the raw coefficient gives a good approximation of the % boost in trade since the exp(ε)-1$\approx\varepsilon$ when ε is near zero.
The partner nations in all datasets are the 14 EU nations (Belgium and Luxembourg's data are fused), Switzerland, Iceland and Norway; the exporting nation is dropped from the list of partners in each regression. The bilateral trade data is taken from the exporting nation (called the 'reporter' in ComTrade jargon).
The GDP coefficients are given in the Appendix to this chapter. The number of observations varies according to the exporting nation, but is over 400,000 in all cases.

The nations listed in the first group of results all use the euro, so the EuroDummy is indicating bilateral trade flows where the euro is a common to the two partners. The raw average (including the negative estimates) is 0.03. Roughly speaking, this says that euro-usage raises the probability of a category switching from zero to a positive flow by about 3%. The figure, however, ranges from about 9% for Ireland to -8% for the Netherlands. For the more geographically peripheral euro area members, the number is 8% or 9%, while it is 1% or 2% for the rest, leaving the Netherlands aside. These statistical results confirm the prima facia evidence presented in Figure 5.4. The main difference is that Table 5.2 results control for fluctuations in the destination nation's GDP, and idiosyncratic, partner-specific factors. It is also worth noting how the results are systematically lower for the three large euro area nations, and it is not statistically different from zero for Germany and Italy. Following the illustrative example at the beginning of the chapter, this could be because many firms were already exporting to the large markets before the euro. To put it differently, the results weakly suggest that the euro made a bigger difference for more firms in the small, peripheral euro area nations.

The second set of results is for nations that are EU members but not in the euro area, so the euro is only used in the destination nation, not the origin nation. Here again we see all positive effects, although only the one for Britain is statistically significant. This provides weak evidence for the idea that euro usage in the importing nation promotes trade in new goods. The size of the effect, as measured by the unweighted average of 2%, is somewhat smaller than of the euro area group.

The final group of results is for the non-EU European nations. Since these countries do not use the euro, the EuroDummy is picking up one-sided euro-usage, again in the importing market. Putting Iceland to the side, the results suggest that euro usage seems to be quite positive for new goods. The point estimates for Switzerland and Norway are positive, significant and similar in size to those of the peripheral euro area nations. Note that these nations are partially in the Single Market due to special agreements with the EU. Norway and Iceland are members of the European Economic Area, which was intended to extend the Single Market to these non-EU members. Switzerland has signed a series of bilateral agreements with the EU that have the same intention.[43]

On the whole, the results in Table 5.2 are supportive of the new goods hypothesis and suggest that nations do not need to use the euro themselves in order for their exporters to benefit in terms of the export of new goods.

5.2.3   Pooled estimations: quasi-intensive margin

The last set of regressions focuses on the euro's impact on the quasi-intensive margin. What we do is drop all categories from each bilateral relationship that have a zero in them at any time. Thus the estimated gravity equation focuses exclusively on goods that were traded before and after the euro. We call this the quasi-intensive margin as there may be some extensive margin involved as well since there may be new goods introduced in categories where trade already existed.

Table 5.3 shows that euro-usage by the importing nation had a positive impact on the trade in categories where trade existed before the euro since we can interpret the point estimates as the percent increase in trade due to the euro. Indeed, all the coefficients that are significant are positive with the exception of Greece. In the euro group, eight of the 11 are positive and significant with coefficients grouped in the 5-10% range. The unweighted average for the whole group is 3%.

The point estimates for the three EU 'outs' are in line with the estimates for the euro area group nations whose coefficients are positive and significant, namely 5-

10%. The estimates for the three non-EU outsiders, however, are not significantly different from zero, although two of the three are estimated as positive.

Table 5.3 Impact of the euro existing trade flows, OLS regressions

Exporter	Euro dummy coefficient	Standard error	p-value
Austria	0.07***	0.0168	0.00
Spain	0.05**	0.0214	0.03
France	0.04***	0.0129	0.00
Ireland	-0.05	0.0304	0.11
Netherlands	0.02*	0.0132	0.10
Portugal	0.13***	0.0233	0.00
Finland	0.06***	0.0128	0.00
Belgium-Luxembourg	0.08***	0.0154	0.00
Italy	0.06***	0.0131	0.00
Germany	-0.01	0.0157	0.66
Greece	-0.12***	0.0336	0.00
Raw Avg	0.03		
UK	0.06***	0.0118	0.00
Denmark	0.09***	0.0147	0.00
Sweden	0.05***	0.0156	0.00
Raw Avg	0.06		
Switzerland	0.00	0.0169	0.83
Iceland	0.11	0.0720	0.11
Norway	-0.01	0.0185	0.58
Raw Avg	0.03		

Notes: Significantly different from zero at ***1% level, ** 5% level, and *10% level.
The estimated equation is:

$$\ln V_{od,i} = c + \beta(EuroDummy_{od}) + \gamma \ln(GDP_d) + time\ dummies + partner\ dummies$$

where $V_{od,i}$ is the bilateral trade flow. This differs from the Table 5.1 results only in the dataset used; here all categories that contain a zero in the bilateral flow for any year are dropped, thus the list of included categories is pair and direction specific (e.g. Germany's exports to France will have a different list than France's exports to Germany).
See Table 5.1 for an explanation of variables.
The partner nations in all datasets are the 14 EU nations (Belgium and Luxembourg's data are fused), Switzerland, Iceland and Norway; the exporting nation is dropped from the list of partners in each regression.
The bilateral trade data is taken from the exporting nation (called the 'reporter' in ComTrade jargon).
The GDP coefficients are given in the Appendix to this chapter. The number of observations varies according to the exporting nation, but is over 400,000 in all cases.

6 Summary and Policy Implications

The costs and benefits of joining the euro area involve a simple trade off according to the traditional view (called the optimal currency area theory, or OCA to cognoscenti):

- The costs come at the macro level. By embracing the ECB's one-size-fits-all policy, the joiner can no longer tailor its monetary policy to national stabilization needs.

- The benefits are at the micro level. By eliminating the national currency, the nation integrates more tightly with the euro area economy and this boosts economic efficiency. A standard gauge of this gain is the trade-enhancing impact of the common currency. A standard story is that the boosted trade is caused by a common-currency-induced reduction in transaction costs among euro area nations.

This report marshals empirical evidence on the size of the micro gains as proxied by the size of the pro-trade effect. Six main findings are extracted from existing empirical research.

(1) The pro-trade effect of the euro (i.e. the Rose effect) is modest – somewhere between 5% and 15%.

(2) It happened very quickly, appearing already in 1999.

(3) It was not exclusive; euro-usage boosted imports from non-euro area nations almost as much as it boosted imports from euro area partners, i.e. there was no trade diversion.

(4) It involved little or no convergence in euro area prices despite the jump in trade flows.

These four findings suggest that the primary driver of the pro-trade effect could not have been a common-currency-induced reduction in transaction costs. If it had been, the extra trade would have been promoted by a quick drop in intra-euro area import prices as the elimination of transaction costs would have acted like a discriminatory trade liberalization among euro area members. These price drops should have: (a) produced trade diversion (since only the euro area 'ins' share the euro); and (b) produced price convergence as the gap between intra-euro area trade prices narrowed. Since there is no evidence for either (a) or (b), it must have been something else. The new evidence presented in this report suggests that the pro-trade effect was caused by the introduction of new goods. This would explain the lack of price convergence (new goods imply higher trade volumes even with constant prices). The report also argues that the mechanism driving trade in new-goods may have been a reduction in the fixed cost of introducing new goods into euro area markets. This mechanism, which is tantamount to a unilateral product-market liberalization, would account for the lack of trade diversion (it would raise the profitability of introducing new goods from euro area-based and non-euro area-based exporters).

(5) The pro-trade effect varies a great deal across nations; Spain seems to have been the biggest gainer while Greece's gain is estimated to be nil or even negative.

(6) The pro-trade effect varies greatly across sectors, with the gains concentrated in increasing-returns-to-scale sectors such as machinery & transport equipment, and chemicals. Beverages & tobacco was the biggest gainer, but this may be due to spurious factors (VAT fraud).

The policy implications of these findings are grouped into two broad categories – lessons for potential joiners and lessons for the euro area's 12 members and its economic management. To share credit where credit is due, I should note that some of the implications I highlight below are stressed by Lane (2006) in his discussion of my draft Chapter 2 (eventually published as Baldwin (2006), but circulated in mid-2005).

6.1 Implications for nations thinking of joining the euro area

Europe's currency union boosted exports of the EU 'outs' to euro area members as well as intra-euro area exports. The best-estimate figures for these 'internal trade creation' and 'external trade creation' effects are 9% for intra-euro area exports and 7% for non-euro area exports to euro area members. Although there is some disagreement among authors on the exact numbers, all researchers find that both numbers are quite low and the gap between them is a few percentage points at most. The implications for potential joiners are straightforward, but perhaps somewhat unexpected.

Because the euro area already exists and encompasses three-quarters of the EU25's GDP, the export prize will be very small for nations who join the euro area. The export gain is limited to the difference between the internal-trade-creation number (9%) and the external-trade-creation' number (7%) and this only with respect to other users of the euro. The joining nation's imports, by contrast, will rise by 9% from its fellow euro area members and 7% from the remaining 'outs'. The straightforward implication of these two facts is that the joiner's imports should rise substantially more than its exports. Indeed, regardless of the overall magnitude of the effects, the lack of trade diversion and the pre-existence of the euro area imply that joiners should experience a larger rise in their imports than in their exports.

Of course, a permanent shift toward current account deficit is not sustainable. The usual general-equilibrium corrective mechanisms would come into play. But focusing narrowly on the trade impact of euro membership, the first round impact would be a greater rise in imports than exports. This result is counter-intuitive if one views reduced transaction costs as the main driver, but this view is not supported by data from the euro area experience. The evidence presented in the report suggests that euro adoption acted as a unilateral product market liberalization. (For completeness, I note that some researchers found that euro-usage boosted both imports and exports of euro area nations. I believe these findings are flawed, but even if they are true the trade effects for joiners is limited to the difference between the internal and external trade effects and so are systematically smaller than estimates of the 'Rose effect' would suggest at first glance.)

Table 6.1 Simulation of extra imports and exports for euro area joiners

	Nations join alone			UK, Sweden and Denmark join together				
Increase in trade (\$ million)	Exports	Total imports	Imports from EA15	Imports from EU 'outs'	Exports	Total imports	Imports from EA15	Imports from EU 'outs'
Britain	2,898	18,490	17,201	1,289	3,728	18,690	18,099	591
Sweden	625	4,129	3,099	1,030	819	4,339	4,047	292
Denmark	360	2,819	2,081	739	764	2,991	2,852	139
	As % of nation's trade with world				*As % of nation's trade with world*			
Britain	1.0%	6.7%			1.3%			6.8%
Sweden	0.8%	5.2%			1.0%			5.4%
Denmark	0.8%	6.3%			1.7%			6.7%

Source: Author's calculations; the point estimates are from Flam and Nordström (2003), Table 6, last column (sample with EU nations only).
Notes: The base year is 2002 and the data source is the IMF DOTS database for bilateral trade (exporters' reports of the flows). The simulation assumes that the joiner's exports to other EA members rise by 2% (9% minus 7%), while its imports from other EA members rise by 9% and imports from non-EA members in the EU rise by 7%. It assumes no change in trade with non-EU nations for simplicity (if the 7% were also applied to third nation exports, the imports change would be large but there would be no additional change in exports).

6.1.1 Britain, Sweden and Denmark free-riding on the euro

To illustrate this point, Table 6.1 works out the implications of the 9% and 7% numbers for the cases of Britain, Sweden and Denmark.

If Britain joined the euro area on its own, the best-estimate figures suggest that UK exports would rise by \$3 billion while imports would rise by \$18 billion. Most of the extra \$18 billion would come from higher exports by existing EA members to Britain, although exports from the rest of the EU outs to Britain are simulated as rising by \$1.2 billion. On the export side, the boost in trade is a modest 1% rise in overall British exports, but an almost 7% rise in imports. The figures for Sweden and Denmark are similar, although of course much smaller given the much smaller base-level of their trade. The extra sales to the euro area would amount to about 1% of total Swedish exports, while the extra sales by EU nations to Sweden would amount to about 5% of total Swedish imports. The corresponding Danish numbers are 1% and 6%.

The right-hand panel of the table simulates the impact of all three joining at once. The impact is broadly similar but the change in exports and imports is more balanced since the export gain to the euro area now applies to three extra nations. The impact is especially marked for Denmark since Danish exports to Britain and Sweden account for a sizeable share of its total exports.

Table 6.1 assumes that external trade creation works only for euro area imports. If membership in the euro area leads to external trade creation on both the export side as well as the import side, as some researchers have found, the prediction of imbalanced trade for joiners is not valid. The bilateral trade with euro area nations would grow by the difference between the internal and external trade creation numbers and trade with third nations would change very little.

A weaker case for joining the euro: Britain, Sweden and Denmark

The lack of trade diversion weakens the political economy case for British, Swedish and Danish membership in the euro area while the small size of the pro-trade effect weakens the economic case. Here is the argument.

The traditional 'optimal currency area' framework is especially relevant to Britain,

Sweden and Denmark. All three have economic management institutions that are capable of running effective independent monetary policies. All three have economies that are large enough and different enough to warrant nationally-tailored monetary policies, at least on occasion. In short, giving up their national currencies would entail a macro cost. This macro cost should be balanced by a micro gain (leaving aside high-politics considerations like greater influence in the EU). A mainstay of such gains stems from trade creation.

The UK Treasury's 2003 study on Britain's readiness to join, for example, suggests that the microeconomic gains from using the euro may be large. HM Treasury (2003) states that: 'a full union of the 15 current EU Member States including the UK could raise trade between members by over 40 per cent'. The report then goes on to suggest that such an increase in trade would boost UK growth and so finds that euro membership would provide large economic gains to Britain. If the real pro-trade effect is just 10%, as suggested by my report, the Treasury's estimates of the economics gains must be scaled back a good deal. Moreover, a good measure of the trade gains – the extra exports to euro area nations – have already occurred, so the gains to Britain from actually adopting the euro are correspondingly reduced. To put it differently, the lack of trade diversion means that the economic case for forming a currency bloc among the major Continental economies is not the same as the case for joining the bloc once it exists.

More specifically, Table 6.1 tells us that the boost in trade from joining the euro area would be modest; this suggests that the case for euro membership is less clear than previously thought. There are two distinct aspects here. Empirical evidence based on the euro's actual effects demonstrates that the trade impact of the euro is more subtle and acts much more like a unilateral trade liberalization than a preferential one. In short, exporters based in the EU 'outs' have had a 'free ride' on the euro area's formation. Moreover, the overall effect, even for the nations that did join is estimated to be small. (HM Treasury (2003), which is otherwise a world-class piece of policy research, uses the 40% trade creation figure that is based on estimates from the pre-euro currency unions; Chapter 2 of this report argues that these estimates are severely flawed and should be ignored for policy purposes.)

Politics versus economics

These numbers suggest a sharp division between the political economy gains and the economic gains from euro membership, but explaining this assertion requires some background. Standard economic analysis tells us that the major gains from trade come from importing. The reason is that importing a good allows the nation to consume at a lower cost. Exports, on the other hand, are basically the price a nation has to pay to enjoy the privilege of importing. Moreover, if markets are fairly competitive, the price a nation receives for its exports reflects the true economic cost of the resources used in making them, so exporting per se is a wash from the welfare perspective. Oversimplifying to make the point, the economic welfare perspective views imports as good and exports as bad.

From a political economy perspective, things are just the other way round. Policy makers often hear from exporters who want improved access to foreign markets and they hear often from domestic firms who want protection from foreign competition. By contrast, consumers who benefit from cheaper imports rarely connect trade policy to the prices they pay in the shops. In this political climate, policies that promote exports are win-win, politically speaking. Policies that promote imports are a hard sell. Or, to put it crudely, exports are good and imports are bad from the political economy perspective.

Looking at things from this angle, the 'news' in Table 6.1 is that the political economy of exports case for membership is much weaker than was suggested in earlier studies. The lack of trade diversion does less, however, to weaken the economic case. euro membership should boost welfare by boosting imports by 5% or 6%. This is a non-negligible figure even if it is only a one-time step up in efficiency.

Continuing on the political economic of trade axis, it should be noted that the big export winners from UK, Swedish and Danish membership would be the euro area nations.

6.1.2   The must-join small members

The traditional view of the costs and benefits of a common currency has little applicability to many of the new members of the EU. These nations are so small that the macroeconomic cost of embracing the euro is not a cost at all. As Buiter and Siebert (2006) put it crisply: 'Their size and openness imply that for the CE8 [the eight Central European newcomers], a national currency is a liability.' This is a common real-world conclusion – one that has led many small nations to abandon their currencies in the past. In Europe, for example, Luxembourg abandoned its national currency in lieu of the Belgian franc, and Monaco to embrace the French franc. Liechtenstein still uses the Swiss franc. As Andres Sutt, deputy governor of the Bank of Estonia said in a July 2005 interview with the Financial Times newspaper: '...you can't cook a different soup in one corner of the pot'.

Table 6.2 Economic size of the 'must join' nations

	GDP at current market prices, million euros	French city with equivalent GDP
Malta	4,483	Dijon
Estonia	10,540	Nice
Latvia	12,789	Lyon
Cyprus	13,418	Lyon
Lithuania	20,587	Marseille
Slovenia	27,373	Marseille + Nice
Luxembourg	28,637	Marseille + Nice

Source: Eurostat online database for 2005 and author's calculations. The French city equivalent uses the national average French GDP per capita and city populations to calculate city GDP.

Table 6.2 makes the point with figures. The GDPs of the six nations most eager to join (listed in the table) are smaller than that of Luxembourg. Indeed, Malta is so small that it makes Luxembourg look like a big economy. For comparison, the table shows French cities whose economies are of comparable size. Just as issuing extra currency in Dijon would do little to stimulate the local economy, pursuing an independent monetary policy in Estonia would do little good and could open the door to a foreign exchange crisis.

Trade effects for the must-join nations

To these nations, the microeconomic gain is tangential to the membership question, but it may be useful to simulate the trade effects of euro area membership.

The results, shown in Table 6.3, yield broadly the same insights as Table 6.1. euro area membership will foster tighter economic integration in the sense of making these nations especially good importers. Their total imports are projected to rise about 10%. They will gain on the export side, but since their exporters have already been benefiting from the single currency in the incumbent euro area nations, the change will only be modest, in the order of a 1% rise in overall exports.

Table 6.3 Simulation of extra imports and exports for likely euro area joiners

	Exports	Total imports		Exports	Total imports
Estonia	46	449	Cyprus	5	245
Lithuania	45	601	Latvia	45	320
Slovenia	117	796	Malta	16	229
	As % of nation's trade with world				
Estonia	1.0%	10.3%	Cyprus	0.1%	5.6%
Lithuania	0.9%	12.2%	Latvia	0.9%	6.5%
Slovenia	1.2%	8.1%	Malta	0.2%	2.3%

Notes: See notes to Table 6.1.

The size of the trade changes are much larger for the Baltic States and Slovenia than they are for Malta and Cyprus because the Mediterranean island states export a smaller fraction of their trade to the euro area.

For completeness, Table 6.4 shows the simulations for the other EU members.

Table 6.4 Simulation of extra imports and exports, other new EU members

	Exports	Total imports		Exports	Total imports
Poland	411	3,358	Bulgaria	56	389
Romania	162	1,070			
Slovak Rep.	155	978			
	As % of nation's trade with world				
Poland	1.4%	8.6%	Bulgaria	1.0%	5.9%
Romania	1.6%	8.6%			
Slovak Rep.	1.1%	6.6%			

Notes: See notes to Table 6.1.

6.2 Implications for the ECB and euro area members: not a silver bullet

The primary motive behind monetary union in Europe was political. Economics played a secondary role. Since the currency union has already been formed and is running rather well, it may seem somewhat amiss to consider the report's findings for monetary union. There are, however, some forward-looking issues where the trade effect of the euro will matter.

6.2.1 Endogenous optimal currency area arguments

Although monetary union was about politics, not economics, one recent line of thinking has cast economics in the role of facilitator. This thinking – the so-called 'endogenous optimal currency area' reasoning – argues that monetary union produces tighter economic integration within the bloc and this makes the ECB's one-size-fits-all monetary policy more appropriate for each of the euro area economies. The pro-trade effect of the euro was one of the key mechanisms suggested. A simple and attractive notion, the endogenous-OCA argument is that sharing a currency would stimulate intra-euro area trade to such an extent that national business cycles would be harmonized. For example, business cycle differences would be evened out by the 'demand spillovers' channel (booming demand in one nation would result in a rapid rise in imports which would in turn stimulate output in other euro area nations).

Plainly this thinking – if it were true – would be very attractive to policy makers in the euro area, the ECB and those Member States who want to join fast. To reform-weary national policy makers in the euro area, this analysis would imply that trade creation is an easy way to harmonize the euro area economically (structural and labour market reforms being the hard way). To potential euro-adopters, it would imply that they need not adjust before joining since trade creation will do the job after joining. To ECB monetary policy deciders, it would hold out the hope that their jobs will get easier.

Alas, the premise is false – at least as far as the trade channel is concerned. This thinking might have been important if the pro-trade effects were as large as the early literature suggested, e.g. Rose (2000). Chapter 2 argues that these large effects were the product of mistaken statistical analysis and that they should be ignored for policy making purposes. The best-estimate of the pro-trade effect is quite modest, so the endogenous-OCA arguments based on trade creation are of second-order importance. A 10% increase in existing trade flows does very little to alter economic integration given the already high level of openness in most EU members.

Of course, other channels such as financial market integration and changes in wage formation processes may still be important empirically, and Lane (2006) marshals evidence that there has been some harmonization of euro area business cycles.

6.2.2   Policy implications

A number of policy implications follow directly from these points.

- Empirical work suggests that the ongoing completion of the Internal Market has done as much or more than the euro in fostering tighter economic integration in Europe. Making the euro area into a more cohesive economic area will require progress on Single Market issues – the pro-trade effects of the common currency will not play a major role.

- Formation of the euro area did boost trade within the group modestly, but enlargement of the euro area to all members of the EU will play almost no role in solving the EA's one-size-fits-all problem. The reason is that the euro has not, as a matter of empirical fact, acted like a custom union formation or free trade agreement. It has not fostered trade on a discriminatory basis but rather promoted euro area imports from all EU members. To the extent that the demand spillovers argument works best when nations trade intensively with each other (as opposed to with third nations), this suggests that euro-induced trade has done little to smooth out national demand shocks. Enlargement of the euro area will do even less.

- The fact that the pro-integration trade channel will provide only modest additional integration serves to emphasize the point that structural and labour market reforms are still necessary.

6.3   Concluding remarks

Adoption of a common currency has undoubtedly had a massive impact on the EU economy. Moreover with only five or six years of data we cannot be confident that our current state of knowledge reflects the true, long-run effects of the euro. What we know as of now, however, alters the fundamental trade-off facing nations that are thinking of joining the euro. Traditionally, a boost in exports is viewed as a political-economy prize to be awarded only to nations that join the euro area. The evidence marshalled in this report suggests that this is not true. The euro has boosted exports to the euro area by euro area members and non-members alike. Moreover, the overall size of the pro-trade effect is modest, in the order of 10%, rather than the much more massive numbers suggested in previous studies and used in, e.g. HM Treasury (2003).

Appendix A: Summary of the most relevant pricing studies

Authors	Estimation	Dependent variable	Data sources	Abstract
Allington, Kattuman, Waldmann (2005)	DID estimation with product fixed effects and nonlinearity in price convergence. Treatment group: EMU.Control group: non-EMU.	Coefficient of variation across prices.	Eurostat. Comparative price level indices for individual consumption expenditure in 200 product groups for all EU countries (1995-2002).	The introduction of the euro was intended to integrate markets within Europe further, after the implementation of the 1992 Single Market Project. Authors examine the extent to which this objective has been achieved, by examining the degree of price dispersion between countries in the euro area, compared to a control group of EU countries outside the euro area. We also establish the role of exchange rate risk in hampering arbitrage by estimating the euro effect for subgroups within the euro area, utilizing differences among eU countries in participation in the Exchange Rate Mechanism. Our results, in contrast with previous empirical research, suggest robustly that the euro has had a significant integrating effect.
Baye et al.(2002)	Linear regression with Euozone and date dummy variables. Controls for product and market structure effects.	Log of average price difference between EMU and non-EMU.	Kelkoo: Prices (normalized to France 10/2002 prices) of a commodity basket of 28 products France, Italy, Netherlands, Spain, Sweden, UK, Denmark. Dates: 10/2001; 12/2001; 01/2002; 05/2002.	Authors study the impact of the Euro on prices charged by online retailers within the EU. Our data spans the period before and after the euro was introduced, covers a variety of products, and includes countries inside and outside of the euro area. Our main finding is that the euro changeover in 2002 neither mitigated price differences nor resulted in purchasing power parity for products sold online. In fact, evidence suggests that online prices in the euro area actually increased compared to prices of EU countries outside the euro area. Further, contrary to the predictions of purchasing-power-parity, we find significant differences in the prices charged by firms both within and across seven countries in the European Union. We also find significant differences in both the average price charged and the best price available in these countries. These conclusions are robust to a variety of controls.
Beck and Weber (2003)	Linear estimate of price volatility as function of the distance between the locations and other explanatory variables. Two sub-periods used to study the effects of the EMU on the size of the estimated border coefficients.	Volatility of the prices of similar goods sold in different locations.	CPI monthly data from 81 locations. Germany (East and West), Austria, Finland, Italy, Spain, Portugal and Switzerland. (January 1991 to December 2002).	Authors use consumer price data for 81 European cities (in Germany, Austria, Finland, Italy, Spain, Portugal and Switzerland) to study the impact of the introduction of the euro on goods market integration. Employing both aggregated and disaggregated consumer price index (CPI) data we confirm previous results which showed that the distance between European cities explains a significant amount of the variation in the prices of similar goods in different locations. We also find that the variation of relative prices is much higher for two cities located in different countries than for two equidistant cities in the same country. Under the EMU, the elimination of nominal exchange rate volatility has largely reduced these border effects, but distance and border still matter for intra-European relative price volatility.

Authors	Estimation	Dependent variable	Data sources	Abstract
Engel and Rogers (2004)	OLS. For each period cross-sectional calculation of mean-squared-error (m.s.e.) of price dispersion. Residual euro effect captured by the unexplained component of m.s.e. (D).1	m.s.e. of relative (logs of) prices.2	Economists Intelligence Unit. Supermarket consumers' prices of 101 traded goods and 38 non-traded items from 18 European cities in 11 euro area countries and 7 cities belonging to non-euro area countries (1990-2003).	Using a detailed dataset of prices of consumer goods in European cities from 1990 to Spring 2003, authors investigate the question of whether the introduction of the euro in January 1999 increased integration of consumer markets as reflected by consumer prices. In fact, we find no tendency for prices to converge after January 1999. This finding holds even when we control for a number of factors that might affect price dispersion. On the other hand, we find that there has been a significant reduction in price dispersion throughout the decade of the 1990s, suggesting that efforts to reduce economic barriers initiated early in the decade may have in fact had the effect of significantly increasing the integration of consumer markets.
Foad(2005)	Pre- and post-EMU relative price volatility calculation. Estimate linear border and distance (dummy variables) effects after correcting for exchange rate volatility.	Average relative price volatility.	US State Department for employees living abroad. Per diem price series of highly non-tradable goods (lodging, meals and incidental expenses) monthly observations covering the period 1/95 to 12/02 for 201 cities in 16 countries.	Has the formation of the European Monetary Union reduced the impact of national borders on cross-border market convergence? This paper extends Engel and Rogers (1996) well known work on border effects to cities across Western Europe over the period 1995-2002 and finds two key results. First, cross-border relative prices tend to be more volatile than prices between locations not separated by a border. This result is robust to a variety of potential explanations for border effects, such as uneven sampling bias, idiosyncratic price shocks, and incomplete exchange rate-pass through. Turning our attention to cross-border price volatility before and after the formation of the EMU, the effects vary by country size. Within the EMU, cross-border price volatility has not changed between the small countries, but has fallen significantly between the large EMU countries.
Friberg and Mathä (2004)	Probit model. One dummy to distinguish if prices in both locations are psychological (PSYCH_SAM)/fractional (FRACT_SAM) and set in euro currency. Another dummy for prices that are both psychological (PSYCH_DIF)/fractional (FRACT_DIF) but set in different currencies. Random effects model.	Price deviation probability. (Probability that price deviation is zero).	Unique price data on a large number of well-specified products from five closely located supermarkets in four different countries (Belgium, France, Germany, Luxembourg) at five occasions before and after the introduction of euro notes and coins (October 2001 to April 2003).	We analyze prices from four countries around the introduction of the Euro. Prices of a good in two locations are more likely to be identical if prices are psychological and set in the same currency. These rounding effects are not important in explaining the size of price differences in the full sample however.

Authors	Estimation	Dependent variable	Data sources	Abstract
Goldberg and Verboven (2004)	Estimation of price differentials function on the speed of convergence and lagged price differentials.Product/country fixed effects introduced. Two sub-periods: 1970-1989 and 1990-2000 to investigate the effect of integration on price dispersion.	The dependent variable is the first difference in the log-price of product i in country k (base country Belgium).	Three dimensional panel containing information on approximately 150 vehicle makes per year in five distinct European markets over the period 1970-2000 for Belgium, France, Germany, Italy and the United Kingdom.	This paper exploits the unique case of European market integration to investigate the relationship between integration and price convergence in international markets. Using a panel dataset of car prices we examine how the process of integration has affected cross-country price dispersion in Europe. We find surprisingly strong evidence of convergence towards both the absolute and the relative versions of the Law of One Price. Our analysis illuminates the main sources of segmentation in international markets and suggests the type of institutional changes that can successfully reduce it.
Imbs et al. (2004)	Fixed effects estimation. Dispersion of prices across European countries (differences in the TV sets' main characteristics are accounted), as a function of distance, volatility, language. EMU dummy included.	1. Log of absolute average price differences for the same TV set across country pairs. 2. Bilateral volatility of relative prices.	GfK France, a private company selling market surveys based on high quality and much disaggregated data. Data on Austria, Belgium, France, Germany, Greece, Italy, the Netherlands, Portugal, Spain, Sweden UK, Hungary, the Czech Republic and Poland and Switzerland. Time period: 1999-2002.	We use a unique dataset on television prices across European countries and regions to investigate the sources of differences in price levels. Our findings are as follows. (i) Quality is a crucial determinant of price differences. (ii) However, sizable international price differentials subsist even for the same television. (iii) EMU countries display lower price dispersion than non-EMU countries. (iv) Price dispersion tends to be smaller regionally than internationally. Regional price dispersion is comparable to intra-EMU dispersion. (v) Absolute price differentials and relative price volatility are positively correlated with exchange rate volatility. (vi) Brand premia and relative rankings of brands differ markedly across borders. (vii) Structural estimates allow a more precise quantification of preference heterogeneity across borders.
Isgut (2002)	OLS model of price dispersion across city pairs determinants. Control variables and EMU dummy included.	The dispersion of goods and services prices between city i and city j	Economist Intelligence Unit's CityData database. Annual observations of domestic currency prices for over 160 goods and services for up to 123 cities during the period 1990-2001.	Using two balanced panels of up to 124 goods and services prices and up to 116 international cities, this paper studies the determinants of price dispersion across city pairs in 2001. Using controls for cities located in the same country, regional trading areas, common languages and historical links, price dispersion increases with geographical distance, nominal bilateral exchange rate volatility, and differences in economic development. Price dispersion is significantly lower across cities located in the euro area. It is also lower for cities that use the US dollar or have currencies hard pegged to it, though the effect is less robust.

Authors	Estimation	Dependent variable	Data sources	Variables
Lutz (2003)	DID approach.Treatment group: EMU.Control group: non-EMU.Control variables: the standard deviation of exchange rate growth, the standard deviation of output growth rates and standard deviation of inflation rates.	Estimated standard deviation of the log of common currency prices.	Four datasets on final goods prices for EU member states. Time interval: 1995-2001.1. Prices of Big Macs that are published annually in The Economist.2. The cover prices of The Economist. 3. Pre-tax car prices from Car Prices in the European Union, a survey of car prices regularly released by the European Commission.4. Data on the costs of various goods and services from Prices and Earnings around the Globe, a publication by the Swiss bank UBS.	This paper examines whether European monetary union has lowered the degree of price dispersion among member countries. A number of different estimation methods are applied to four independent datasets containing prices of identical goods. While the results reported in the paper vary somewhat across goods, they provide little overall support of the European Commission's claim that the single currency would significantly deepen market integration among the Eurozone countries. Even though this should be viewed as preliminary evidence, it does suggest that there are other, more important impediments to market integration in the EU.
Mathä (2003)	1. Random effects estimation of prices deviations on distance. Border and monetary association dummy included.2. OLS between and product specific fixed effects.	Absolute percentage price difference one product between two different locations.	Price data on 6 different supermarkets, on 92 products collected at four different points in time: mid-October 2001, mid-December 2001, mid-February 2002, and mid-April 2002.	This paper uses individual supermarket prices and analyzes to what extent absolute deviations from the law of one price are attributable to transaction costs. The results indicate that absolute percentage price differences are increasing in distance, but at a decreasing rate. Similarly, crossing borders increases price deviations, while being inside the former Belgian-Luxembourg monetary association has the opposite effect. This result nurtures the hopes that the euro may be able to reduce regional and cross-border price differences in the long term. Furthermore, larger differences in packaging sizes result in larger price deviations, while the opposite is the case for prices observed within the same retail group.
Parsley and Wei (2001)	Linear regression of prices dispersion on a set of independent variables as distance, instrumental (i.e. tariff rates) and institutional (i.e. trade blocks) variables. City and time fixed effects. Euro dummy included.	Standard deviation of prices.	Economist Intelligence Unit. Panel dataset of 95 goods and 83 cities (one city per country) during 1990-2000.	This paper studies the effects of instrumental and institutional stabilization exchange rate volatility on the integration of goods markets. Rather than using data on volume of trade, this paper employs tri-dimensional panel of prices of 95 very disaggregated goods in 83 cities around the world during 1990-2000. Authors find that the impact of an institutional stabilization promotes market integration far beyond an instrumental stabilization. Among them, long-term currency unions are more effective than more recent currency boards. All have room to improve relative to a US benchmark.

Authors	Estimation	Dependent variable	Data sources	Variables
Rogers (2002)	Price dispersion relation with harmonization of tax rates, convergence of incomes and labour costs, liberalization of trade and factor markets, and increased coherence of monetary policy, measures as the cross-country standard deviation of the average monthly change in each country's exchange rate versus the European currency basket (ECU, then Euro) in year t.	Standard deviation of prices across cities for a certain product.	Economist Intelligence Unit (EIU).Data from 25 European cities - from all 12 current Euro area members and five other nations - and 13 US cities. The data are annual from 1990 to 2001.	In light of 50 years of economic policies designed to integrate Europe it is of interest to assess how far European integration has come in practice. Using a unique dataset, I document the pattern of price dispersion across European and US cities from 1990 to 2001. I find a striking decline in dispersion for traded goods prices in Europe, most of which took place between 1991 and 1994. The level of traded goods price dispersion in the Euro area is now quite close to that of the United States. A decline in dispersion of non-tradable prices in Europe has also taken place, but to a smaller extent. For US cities, there is no evidence of a decline in price dispersion, even for tradable. The author examines several possible explanations for the decline in European price dispersion. Including harmonization of tax rates, convergence of incomes and labour costs, liberalization of trade and factor markets, and increased coherence of monetary policy. The author also investigate how much of the variation in national inflation rates in Europe can be explained by price level convergence.
Wolszczak-Derlacz (2004)	Regression of the Relative price level on GDP per capita, labour and transportation costs.	Relative price level which is equal to the ratio between the PPP and the exchange rate.	Eurostat and Economic Intelligence Unit.	The article examines the price dispersion in the European Union in the last ten years. The analysis is based on the relative price level (RPL) which is the ratio between Purchasing Power Parity (PPP) and exchange rate. RPL is interpreted in relation to the average price level of EU (EU15-100). The analysis of price convergence is examined on the aggregate and disaggregates level. Moreover the regression between RPL and GDP per capita, labour costs and transportation cost is tested to measure the contribution of different factors in explaining the observed convergence pattern.

Notes: Table prepared by my graduate student Nadia Rocha.
[1] m.s.e decomposed in: time invariant component (A), time-varying equilibrium price component (B), slow price adjustment component (C), unexplained component (D).
[2] Positive value means a decrease in price dispersion.

Appendix B: GDP estimates from the regressions

Coefficients on Partner GDP in the three sets of regressions

	Tobit coefficient	std. Error	P. value	OLS coefficient	std. Error	P. value	Logit coefficient	std. Error	P. value
Austria	1.125718	0.084846	0	0.256491	0.058078	0	0.454306	0.03481	0
Belgium-Luxembourg	0.693204	0.076421	0	0.168321	0.054484	0.002	0.238142	0.035488	0
Switzerland	0.851839	0.069018	0	0.222631	0.051959	0	0.38054	0.031088	0
Germany	0.956099	0.077575	0	0.29692	0.050067	0	0.307064	0.028874	0
Denmark	1.133631	0.066913	0	0.208168	0.046493	0	0.442894	0.028388	0
Spain	0.77988	0.106688	0	-0.2517	0.072215	0	0.303053	0.035359	0
Finland	0.879662	0.056447	0	0.463831	0.042136	0	0.351232	0.033417	0
France	0.107173	0.054026	0.047	0.283438	0.035525	0	-0.1423	0.034158	0
UK	0.816739	0.05259	0	0.247477	0.039177	0	0.500759	0.033034	0
Greece	1.451512	0.130903	0	0.62797	0.09754	0	0.475032	0.04915	0
Ireland	1.162174	0.180277	0	0.077645	0.106596	0.466	0.374036	0.050945	0
Island	1.269528	0.354842	0	0.505928	0.246746	0.04	0.382519	0.115587	0.001
Italy	1.020556	0.061295	0	0.352261	0.043663	0	0.434146	0.031639	0
Netherlands	1.059987	0.059839	0	0.398672	0.040352	0	0.419303	0.027305	0
Norway	0.712243	0.09147	0	0.137699	0.067261	0.041	0.27493	0.036451	0
Portugal	1.029709	0.115189	0	0.238504	0.075208	0.002	0.330389	0.03737	0
Sweden	0.753967	0.074005	0	0.224579	0.051199	0	0.259905	0.029125	0

Source: Author's calculations

Endnotes

1   See *http://www.econlib.org/library/Enc/GoldStandard.html.*

2   Published in 1991 as 'On the Microeconomics of the European Monetary Union'.

3   Bini Smaghi (1991).

4   Jeffery Frankel has posted photos of the event at *http://ksghome.harvard.edu/~jfrankel/ECB%20June2005pixJF&RB.htm.* His unedited comment is at *http://ksghome.harvard.edu/~jfrankel/BaldwinECB-RoseEffectdAug05.pdf.*

5   Standard references for the gravity model are Tinbergen (1962), Pöyhönen (1963a), Linnemann (1966), Anderson (1979), Bergstrand (1985) and Helpman and Krugman (1985). It was reintroduced to US academic circles by McCallum (1995) and Frankel and Wei. (1993).

6   I believe the Rose trade data has a systematic bias in it, what I call the silver-medal mistake below.

7   This section is based on Baldwin and Taglioni (2006); see that paper for a more formal treatment of the theory and econometrics.

8   See Baldwin and Taglioni (2006), or the original presentation by Anderson and van Wincoop (2001).

9   See Jeffery Frankel's discussion in Baldwin (2006) for an account of why no one before Rose asked the currency union question empirically.

10 Note that when Glick and Rose (2002) run their regression without the time dummies, their estimated coefficient on the CU dummy is one standard deviation larger than it is with time dummies, so it can be important to correct the small problem.

11 In his chapter on the gravity model, Feenstra (2003) shows an equation with the log of the sums, rather than the sum of the logs. The theory leading up to this, however, is developed in the context of the simplest trade model - i.e. the Krugman trade model without trade costs. In this model, all bilateral flows are identical so the sum of the logs does equal the log of the sums. However, when trade costs are introduced, the theory does not necessarily predict bilaterally balanced trade; real-world trade flows are often very unbalanced, especially between big and small nations.

12 If $x = y\delta$, $\ln[(x + y)/2] = \ln x + \ln(1+\delta) - \ln 2$, while $\ln(xy\delta)/2 = \ln(x) + \ln(\delta)/2$. The wrong way minus the right way is $\ln(1+\delta) - \ln\delta/2 - \ln 2$; this difference gets large as δ deviates from unity.

13 Formally, if one asks the statistics whether the country dummies should be excluded from Rose-Wincoop, the answer is no. They belong. Therefore, the Rose effect estimates performed without them are null and void.

14 Bill Bryson, in his book *Mother Tongue*, claims that this aphorism is ancient, so that we should read 'proves' using its archaic meaning, 'tests', as in proving grounds.

15 Glick and Rose (2001) show a figure for Anglo-Irish that looks quite different; they use the level of trade which drops due the second oil-shock recession. Thom and Walsh look at the bilateral trade as a share of all Irish exports and thus control somewhat for the global recession.

16 Note that Rose (2000) does roughly this with his difference-in-difference regression that is reported in the text but not in a table; the Rose effect this yields is only 17% more trade.

17 By the way, these suspicions of mine were raised by the similarity of the two different techniques applied on two separate datasets. It would be interesting to make a more direct comparison, to see what the Rose-Wincoop country-dummy technique would yield on the Glick-Rose dataset, and what the Glick-Rose pair dummy technique would yield on the Rose-Wincoop dataset. Such comparisons would help us to judge the importance of the omitted variable critique, and the validity of the Glick-Rose solution of throwing in one pair dummy for the whole period.

18 Actually you can see it, since *Economic Policy* posts the Panel drafts on its website: www.economic-policy.org.

19 By the way, this nonlinearity is consistent with Krugman's famous Home Market Effect whereby a nation's exports are affected by its size.

20 It would be interesting to see the share of trade pairs with common currencies by year, but this is not reported in Glick-Rose; only the full panel average is reported.

21 See Baldwin and Robert-Nicoud (2002) for an explanation based on sunk costs.

22 Tenreyro has a recent paper on the impact of exchange volatility on trade that applies the same IV strategy. Her conclusion is that volatility has no effect on trade, which is strange given her early findings on the CU dummy. Strangely, this paper, Tenreyro (2001), excludes the common currency variable altogether and indeed never mentions it. Maybe it would have been too jarring to have a common currency boosting trade many times over, but lower volatility having no impact. Or, maybe she, like Rose, decided that IV estimation of the Rose effect was a dead end.

23 Actually, since France includes some small, poor, open and remote islands (Outré-Mers), we could test whether the euro boosted trade between these islands and the nations that were not in the DM bloc-franc fort complex, say, Greece, Portugal, Spain, Finland and Ireland.

24 This literature review draws on Gomes et al. (2004).

25 Here is Andy's email to me (I was a Managing Editor of *Economic Policy* at the time): 'Respected Editors, Ernesto Stein (and co-authors) at the IADB has just started to circulate a short paper which analyzes the effect of EMU on intra-EMU trade using data from the first couple of years of EMU. He shows the effect is significant (about 15-25% after just two years), using only data from the EU15 and also a larger sample of developed countries. I'm obviously biased (though I should say that I'm trying to escape this particular sub-literature). But it's of obvious policy relevance for Europe and the ancestors of his work appear in *Economic Policy*, so I think it's of potential interest to you. Anyway, now that I've alerted you to it, I've done my duty to God and the Queen.'

26 Full disclosure: I was the Managing Editor who did the rewriting. I probably should have already mentioned that Andy Rose and I were PhD classmates at MIT 1982-86.

27 MSO, like many authors in this literature, use EMU to stand for 'European monetary union'; unfortunately, EMU stands for 'Economic and Monetary Union' - at least since the Maastricht Treaty that implemented EMU in both correct and incorrect senses. All EU members are part of EMU, so writers who are familiar with European integration use the terms euro area, Euroland or euro area to refer to those EU members who have adopted the euro. Also EA is shorter than EMU.

28 Just to take one example, the EU signed dozens of preferential trade agreements during the 1992-2002 period. Since each of these erodes the preference margin of EU members, they should alter intra-EU trade flows.

29 In fact, MSO should probably have used 1993-2002 data since the new data collection systems started with 1993 data.

30 The pair dummies are time-invariant and thus miss part of the Anderson-van Wincoop point of using time-varying country dummies, but given the short period, one can hope that the omission is not too important. Moreover, someone should redo MSO's estimates with time-varying country dummies (obviously in this case one cannot also include pair dummies).

31 Note that MSO try to control for the observable part of this, but the measure they use is extremely crude and so surely fails to fully control for this. See *http://europa.eu.int/comm/internal_market/score/index_en.htm.*

32 More formally, MSO statistically reject the pooling hypothesis that would be necessary for the estimates without dummies to make sense.

33 They write: 'If dollar prices of goods produced in the euro area fall as a result of depreciation, the value of trade between two EMU countries will fall as well, relative to trade between other countries, and the EMU effect on trade could potentially be underestimated. One way to deal with this issue would be to control for bilateral unit value indices in order to capture the change in import and export prices. Unfortunately, these indices are not available. For this reason, in order to control for these valuation effects we include in most regressions an index of the real exchange rate for each of the countries in the pair (the index is the ratio between the nominal exchange rate of each country vis-à-vis the US dollar and the country's GDP deflator). Reassuringly, the inclusion of these indices does not change the results significantly.'

34 Their pair dummies correct for the relative-prices-matter term on average but Anderson-VanWinccop showed us that this term should vary over time; moreover, the relative-prices-matter term definitely includes bilateral exchange rates between the USA and each importing nation so a spurious correlation is assured.

35 Forcing the pair dummy to be the same for a half century is a bit strained, although all authors using the Glick-Rose data do this. For example, surely the Franco-German dummy was strongly negative in the first part of the sample and strongly positive in the last part. It would be interesting to see what happens if they allow, for example, decadal pair dummies.

36 This idea was to figure out how much of Britain's superior macro performance was due to their decision to stay out of the euro area, but with so few data points this proved elusive.

37 The numbers for Greece, Portugal and Finland are not significantly different to zero, except Greece's EA1 estimate which is significant at the 5% level of confidence.

38 To be more precise, the demand equation is $X_{od} = n_o(p_{od}/P_d)^{-\sigma}(E_d/P_d)$ where X_{od} is the volume of o's exports to d.

39 In particular the impact will be multiplied by nation-i's expenditure share in nation-d's market.

40 ComTrade doesn't report non-traded goods (zeros); it was possible to square the database by inserting categories for which a nation has exported at least once to at least one destination, but not included are those categories which never exported to anyone during the period considered.

41 Dividing this total we see that there are about 2,500 zeros in the average outsider export vector to the average EA nation. This means about half the possible goods are not exported, although of course the number varies by market (there are far fewer zeros in Switzerland's export vector to Germany than its export vector to Portugal, for example).

42 That is, the time dummies and the constant will be perfectly collinear with any nation-o variable.

43 Norway and Iceland are in the European Economic Area and Switzerland has bilateral agreements with the EU, but these do not grant full Single Market status. For example, the lack of a customs union with the EU means that this trade is subject to distortionary rules of origin.

References

Alesina, A., Barro, R.J. and Tenreyro, S. (2002), 'Optimal Currency Areas', Harvard Institute Research Working Paper No. 1958, June.

Alho, K. (2002), 'The Impact of Regionalism on Trade in Europe', Royal Economic Society Annual Conference 2003, 3, Royal Economic Society.

Allington, N., Kattuman, P. and Waldmann, F. (2005), 'One Market, One Money, One Price?', *International Journal of Central Banking*, 2005, pp. 73-115.

Anderson, J. E. (1979), 'A Theoretical Foundation for the Gravity Equation', *American Economic Review*, 69(1), pp. 106-16.

Anderson, J. and van Wincoop, E. (2001), 'Gravity with Gravitas: A Solution to the Border Puzzle', NBER Working Paper No. 8079, January.

Anderton, R., Baltagi, B., Skudelny, F. and De Souza, N. (2002) 'Intra- and Extra-Euro Area Import Demand for Manufactures', European Trade Study Group Annual Conference, 2002, 4, European Trade Study Group.

Anderton, R., Baldwin, R. and Taglioni, D. (2003), 'The Impact of Monetary Union on Trade Prices', ECB Working Paper No. 238, June.

Andrews, D.W.K. (2003), 'End-of-Sample Instability Tests', *Econometrica*, 71(6), pp. 1661-94.

Artis, M.J. (2002), 'Reflections on the Optimal Currency Area (OCA) criteria in the light of EMU', Oesterreichische Nationalbank Working Paper No. 69, July.

Artis, M. and Zhang, W. (1995), 'International Business Cycles and the ERM: Is There a European Business Cycle?', CEPR Discussion Paper No. 1191.

Asplund, M. (2002), 'Risk Averse Firm in Oligopoly', *International Journal of Industrial Organization*.

Augier, P., Gasiorek, M. and lai Tong, C. (2005), 'The Impact of Rules of Origin on Trade Flows', *Economic Policy*, 20(43), pp. 567-624.

Baldwin, R. (1991), 'On the Microeconomics of the European Monetary Union', European Economy, Special Issue No. 1, 'One Market, One Money', European Commission, Brussels.

Baldwin R. (2005), 'Heterogeneous Firms: Testable and Untestable Properties of the Melitz Model', NBER Working Paper No. 11471, May.

Baldwin, R. (2006), 'The euro's trade effect', ECB Working Paper 594, March.

Baldwin, R. and Di Nino, V. (2006), 'Testing for the Euro's Impact on the Extensive Margin of Trade: What Do We Learn From Zeros?', HEI manuscript, March.

Baldwin, R. and Robert Nicoud, F. (2002), 'Entry and Assymetric Lobbying: Why Governments Pick Losers', NBER Working Paper No.8756.

Baldwin, R. and Taglioni, D. (2005), 'Positive OCA Criteria: Microfoundations for the Rose Effect', March (*http://hei.unige.ch/~baldwin/TradeEffectsEuroBaldwin.html*).

Baldwin R. and Taglioni, D. (2006), 'Gravity for dummies and Dummies for Gravity (Equations)', manuscript.

Baldwin, R., Bertola, G. and Seabright, P. (2003), *EMU: Assessing the Impact of the Euro*, Blackwell Publishing Ltd, Oxford.

Baldwin, R., Skuderlny, F. and Taglioni, D. (2005), 'Trade Effects of the Euro: Evidence from Sectoral Data', European Central Bank, Working Paper No. 446.

Barr, D., Breedon, F. and Miles, D. (2003), 'Life on the Outside', *Economic Policy*, 18, pp. 573-613.

Baye, M., Gatti, R., Kattuman, P. and Morgan, J. (2002), 'Online Pricing and the Euro Changeover: Cross Country Comparisons', Judge Institute of Management Working Paper 17 (forthcoming in *Economic Inquiry*).

Beck, G. and Weber, A. (2003), 'How Wide are European Borders? On the Integration Effects of Monetary Unions', Center of Financial Studies Economic Paper No. 2001/07, Revisited.

Berger, H. and Nitsch, V. (2005), 'Zooming Out: The Trade Effect of the Euro in Perspective', CESifo Working Paper No. 1435.

Bergin, A., Fitz Gerald, J. and McCoy, D. (2004), 'How Has Economic Management Evolved Within EMU', Paper presented at the Annual Kenmare Economic Workshop, October, http://www.esri.ie/pdf/Economic_Wkshop_Oct04.pdf.

Bergstrand, J. (1985), 'The Gravity Equation in International Trade: Some Microeconomic Foundations and Empirical Evidence', *Review of Economics and Statistics*, 67(3), pp. 474-81.

Bernard, A.B., Eaton, J., Jenson, J.B. and Kortum, S. (2000), 'Plants and Productivity in International Trade', NBER Working Paper No. 7688.

Bernard, A. and Jensen, B. (2004), 'Exporting and Productivity in the USA', *Oxford Review of Economic Policy*, 20(3).

Bini-Smaghi, L. (1991), 'Exchange Rate Variability and International Trade: Why is it so Difficult to Find any Empirical Relationship?', *Applied Economics*, 23, pp. 927-36.

Buiter, W. and Sibert, A. (2006), 'Eurozone Entry of New EU Member States from Central Europe: Should They? Could They?', *http://www.nber.org/~wbuiter/eurozone.pdf*.

Bun Maurice, J.B. and Klaassen, F. (2002), 'Has the Euro increased Trade?', Tinbergen Institute Discussion Papers, TI 2002 108-2, October.

Bun Maurice, J.B. and Klaassen, F. (2004), 'The Euro Effect on Trade is not as Large as Commonly Thought', Tinbergen Institute Discussion Papers No. 2003-086/2, October.

De Nardis, S. and Vicarelli, C. (2003a), 'The Impact of Euro on Trade: The (Early) Effect is not so Large', European Network of Economic Policy Research Institutes, Working Paper No. 017.

De Nardis, S. and Vicarelli, C. (2003b), 'Currency Unions and Trade: The Special Case of EMU', *World Review of Economics*, 139(4), 625-49.

De Souza, L.V. (2002), 'Trade Effects of Monetary Integration in Large, Mature Economies', A Primer on European Monetary Union, Kiel Working Paper No. 1137.

De Souza, J. and Lamotte, O. (2006), 'Does Political Disintegration Lead to Trade Disintegration? Evidence from Former Yugoslavia', Manuscript.

Deardorff, A. (1998), 'Determinants of Bilateral Trade: Does Gravity Work in a Neoclassical World?', in Jeffrey Frankel (ed.), *The Regionalization of the World Economy*, University of Chicago Press.

Dell'Arricia, G. (1998), 'Exchange Rate Fluctuations and Trade Flows: Evidence from the European Union', IMF Working Paper No. WP98/107.

Devereux, Michael B. and Lane, Philip R. (2003), 'Understanding Bilateral Exchange Rate Volatility', *Journal of International Economics* 60, pp. 109-132.

Engel, C. and Rogers, J.H. (2004), 'European Product Market Integration after the Euro', *European Policy* 19(39), pp. 347.

European Commission (1990) 'One Market, One Money', *European Economy* 44.

European Commission (2000), 'Report from the Commission to the Council and the European Parliament', COM(2000), 28 final.

European Commission (2004), 'The Internal Market Index 2004', DG Joint Research, July, available at *http://webfarm.jrc.cec.eu.int/uasa/doc/Tarantola/IMI_2004/ The%20Internal%20Market%20Index%202004.pdf*.

Evenett, S.J. and Wolfang, K. (2002), 'On Theories Explaining the Success of the Gravity Equation', *Journal of Political Economy* 110, pp. 281-316 .

Feenstra, R. (2003), *Advanced International Trade*, Princeton University Press, Princeton, NJ.

Fidrmuc, J. and Fidrmuc, J. (2003), 'Disintegration and Trade', *Review of International Economics*, 11, p. 811.

Flam H. and Nordström, H. (2003) 'Trade Volume Effects of the Euro: Aggregate and Sector Estimates', Institute for International Economic Studies, unpublished.

Foad, H. (2005), 'Europe without Borders? The Effect of the EMU on Relative Prices', available at *http://ssrn.com/abstact=514502*.

Frankel, J.A. (1997), *Regional Trading Blocs in the World Economic System*, Institute for Internal Economics, Washington, DC.

Frankel J. (2003), 'The UK Decision RE EMU. Implications of Currency Blocs for Trade and Business Cycle Correlations', in Submissions on EMU from Leading Academics, HM Treasury, London, pp. 99-109.

Frankel, J.A. and Rose, A.K. (1996), 'The Endogeneity of the Optimum Currency Area Criteria', NBER Working Paper No. 5700.

Frankel, J.A. and Rose, A.K. (1998), 'The Endogeneity of the Optimum Currency Area Criteria', *Economic Journal*, 108, July, pp. 1009-25.

Frankel, J.A. and Rose, A.K. (2000), 'Estimating the Effect of Currency Unions on Trade and Output', NBER Working Paper No. 7857, August.

Frankel, J. and Wei, S-j. (1993), 'Trade Blocs and Currency Blocs', NEBR Working Paper No. W4335.

Friberg, R. and Mathä, T.Y. (2004), 'Does a Common Currency Lead to (More) Price Equalisation? The Role of Psychological Pricing Points', *Economic Letters*, 84, pp. 281-7.

Gagnon, J.E. (2003), 'Long-Run Supply Effects and the Elasticities Approach', FRB International Finance Discussion Paper No. 754.

Glick, R. and Rose, A. (2001), 'Does a Currency Union Affect Trade? The Time Series Evidence', *European Economic Review*, 46(6), pp. 1125-51.

Goldberg, P.K. and Knetter, M.M. (1997), 'Goods Prices and Exchange Rates: What Have We Learned?', *Journal of Economic Literature*, 35(3), pp. 1243-72.

Goldberg, P. and Verboven, F. (2004), 'Market Integration and Convergence to the Law of One Price: Evidence from the European Car Market', *Journal of International Economics*, 65(1), pp. 49-73.

Gomes, T., Graham, C., Helliwell, J., Kano, T., Murray, J. and Schembri, L. (2004), 'The Euro and Trade: Is there a Positive Effect?', pdf file of a preliminary and incomplete draft, not for quotation without permission.

Harrigan, J. (2001), 'Specialization and the Volume of Trade: Do the Data Obey the Laws?', NBER Working Paper No. 8675, December.

Helpman, E. and Krugman, P. (1985), *Market Structure and Foreign Trade*, MIT Press.

Helpman, E., Melitz, M. and Rubinstein, Y. (2005), 'Trading Partners and Trading Volumes', Preliminary and Incomplete, 31 March .

HM Treasury (2003), 'EMU and Trade', Background Study for the UK Treasury's Assessment on the euro, available at *http://www.tcd.ie/iiis/pages/publications/discussionpapers/IIISDP115.php*.

Hummels, D., Ishii, J. and Yi, K. (2001), 'The Nature and Growth of Vertical Specialization in World Trade', *Journal of International Economics*, 54, 75-96.

Imbs, J., Mumtaz, H., Ravn, M.O. and Rey, H. (2004), 'Price Convergence: What's on TV?', Mimeo.

IMF (International Monetary Fund) (1984), 'Exchange Rate Volatility and World Trade: A Study by the Research Department of the IMF', IMF Occasional Paper, No. 28, International Monetary Fund, Washington, July.

Isgut, A. (2002), 'Common Currencies and Market Integration across Cities: How Strong is the Link?', in *Financial Development and Stability*, Oxford University Press, Chapter 8.

Kenen, P.B. (2002), 'Currency Unions and Trade: Variations on Themes by Rose and Persson', Reserve Bank of New Zealand Discussion Paper 2002/08.

Klaassen, F. (2004), 'Why is it so Difficult to Find an Effect on Exchange Rate Risk on Trade?', *Journal of International Money and Finance*, 23(5), pp. 817-39.

Krugman, P. (1989), 'Differences in Income Elasticities and Trends in Real Exchange Rates', *European Economic Review,* 33, pp. 1055-85.

Krugman, P. (1993), 'Lesson from Massachusetts for EMU', in Torres F. and Giavazzi, F. (eds), *Adjustment and Growth in the European Monetary Union*, Cambridge University Press, Cambridge.

Lane, P. (2006), 'The Real Effects of EMU', IIIS Discussion Paper No. 115.

Levy, Y.E. (2003) 'On the Impact of Common Currency on Bilateral Trade', *Economics Letters*, 79, pp. 125-9.

Linnemmann, H. (1966), An Econometric Study of International Trade Flows, North-Holland, Amsterdam.

Lutz, M. (2003), 'Price Convergence under EMU? First Estimates', Discussion Paper No. 2003-08, Department of Economics, University of St Gallen, Switzerland.

Mancini-Griffoli, T. and Pauwels, L. (2006), 'Is There a Euro Effect on Trade? An Application of End-of-Sample Structural Break Tests for Panel Data', HEI manuscript.

Markusen, J. and A. Venables (2000), 'The General Theory of Inter-Industry-, Intra-Industry-, and Multinational Trade', *Journal of International Economics*, 52, 209-34 .

Mathä, T. (2003), 'What to Expect of the Euro? Analysing Price Differences of Individual Products in Luxembourg and its Surrounding Regions', Mimeo, Banque Centrale de Luxembourg.

McCallum, J. (1995), 'National Borders Matter: Canada-US Regional Trade Patterns', *The American Economic Review*, 85(3), pp. 615-23.

Melitz J. (2001), 'Geography, Trade and Currency Union', CEPR Discussion Paper No. 2987, October.

Melitz, M. (2003), 'The Impact of Trade on Intraindustry Reallocations and Aggregate Industry Productivity', *Econometrica*, 71, pp. 1695-725.

Melitz, M.J. and Ottaviano, G.I.P. (2003), 'Market Size, Trade and Productivity', June, 6.

Micco, A., Stein, E. and Ordoñez, G. (2003a), 'The EMU Effect on Trade: What's in it for the UK?', Inter-American Development Bank, July.

Micco, A., Stein, E. and Ordoñez, G. (2003b), 'The Currency Union Effect on Trade: Early Evidences from EMU', *Economic Policy*, 37, October, pp. 317-56.

Mongelli, P., Dorrucci, E. and Agur, I. (2005), 'What Does European Institutional Integration Tell Us About Trade Integration?', ECB Occasional Paper, 40.

Mundell, R.A. (1961), 'A Theory of Optimum Currency Areas', *The American Economic Review*, 51(4), pp. 657-65.

Neary, J.P. and Leahy, D. (2000), 'Strategic Trade and Industrial Policy towards Dynamic Oligopolies', *Economic Journal*, 110(463), pp. 484-508.

Nitsch, V. (2002), 'Honey I Shrunk the Currency Union Effect on Trade', *World Economy*, 25(4), pp. 457-74.

Obstfeld, M. and Rogoff, K. (2000), 'The Six Major Puzzles in International Macroeconomics: Is there a Common Cause?', NBER Macroeconomics Annual 2000, MIT Press.

Pakko, M.R. and Wall, H.J. (2001), 'Reconsidering the Trade-Creating Effects of a Currency Union', Federal Reserve Board of St Louis Review, 83(5), 37-45.

Parsley, D.C. and Shang-jin, W. (2001), 'Limiting Currency Volatility to Stimulate Goods Market Integration', NBER Working Paper No. 8468.

Persson, T. (2001), 'Currency Unions and Trade: How Large is the Treatment Effect?', *Economic Policy*, 33, October, pp. 435-48.

Piscitelli, L. (2003), Mimeo, UK Treasury.

Pöyhönen, P. (1963a), 'A Tentative Model for the Volume of Trade Between Countries', *Welwirtschaftliches Archiv*, 90(1), 93-9.

Pöyhönen, P. (1963b), 'Toward a General Theory of International Trade', Ekonomiska *Samfundets Tidskrift*, 16(2), 69-78.

Rocha, N. (2006), 'Fixed Trade Cost Liberalization in a Multi-Nation World: Rose Effect without Trade Diversion', GIS manuscript, PhD.

Rogers, J. (2002), 'Monetary Union, Price Level Convergence, and Inflation: How Close is Europe to the United States?', International Finance Discussion Paper No. 740, Board of Governors of the Federal Reserve System, Washington, DC .

Rose, A.K. (1999), 'One Money, One Market: Estimating the Effect of Common Currencies on Trade', CEPR Working Paper No.7432, December.

Rose, A.K. (2000a), 'One Money, One Market: Estimating the Effect of Common Currencies on Trade', *Economic Policy*, 30, 7-46.

Rose, A.K. (2000b), 'EMU's Potential Effect on British Trade: A Quantitative Assessment', 4 July.

Rose, A.K. (2001a), 'Currency Unions and Trade: The Effect is Large', *Economic Policy*, 33, pp. 449-61.

Rose, A.K. (2001b), 'EMU and Swedish Trade', 9 November.

Rose, A.K. (2002), 'Honey the Currency Union Effect on Trade hasn't blown up', *The World Economy*, 25(4), April.

Rose, A. and Stanley, D. (2004), 'A Meta-Analysis of the Effect of Common Currencies on International Trade', *Journal of Economic Surveys*, 19, p. 347.

Rose, A.K. and van Wincoop, E. (2000), 'National Money as a Barrier to International Trade: The Real Case for Currency Union', *http://faculty.haas.berkeley.edu/arose/*.

Rose, A.K. and van Wincoop, E. (2001), 'National Money as a Barrier to Trade: The Real Case for Monetary Union', *American Economic Review*, 91(2), 386-90.

Ruffles, D., Tily J. and Caplan, D. (2003), 'VAT Missing Trader Intra-Community Fraud: The effect on Balance of Payments Statistics and UK National Accounts', *www.statistics.gov.uk/articles/economic_trends/ETAug03Ruffles.pdf*.

Silva, S. and Tenreyro, S. (2003), 'Gravity-Defying Trade', Federal Reserve Bank of Boston Working Paper No. 03-01, 9 January.

Taglioni, D. (2002), 'Exchange Rate Volatility as a Barrier to Trade: New Methodologies and Recent Evidence', *Open Economies Review* 7, pp. 493-499.

Tenreyro, S. (2001), 'On the Causes and Consequences of Currency Unions', Harvard University, Mimeo.

Tenreyro, S. and Barro, R.J. (2003), 'Economic Effects of Currency Unions', NBER Working Paper 9435.

Thom, R. and Walsh, B. (2002), 'The Effect of a Currency Union on Trade: Lessons From the Irish Experience', *European Economic Review*, 46, pp. 1111-23.

Tinbergen, J. (1962), *Shaping the World Economy: Suggestions of an International Economic Policy*, New York: The Twentieth Centiry Fund.

Wei, S-J. (1999), 'Currency Hedging and Goods Trade', *European Economic Review*, 43, pp. 1371-94.

Wolszczak-Derlacz, J. (2004), 'One Europe, One Product, Two Prices: The Price Disparity in the EU', Paper presented at the 3rd International Conference of the EEFS, 'World Economy and European Integration' University of Gdansk, Sopot, 13-16 May.

Wyplosz, C. (1997), 'EMU: Why and How it May Happen?', *Journal of Economic Perspectives*, 11, Fall, pp. 3-22.

Yi, K. (2003), 'Can Vertical Specialization Explain Growth of World Trade?', *Journal of Political Economy*, February, pp. 52-102.